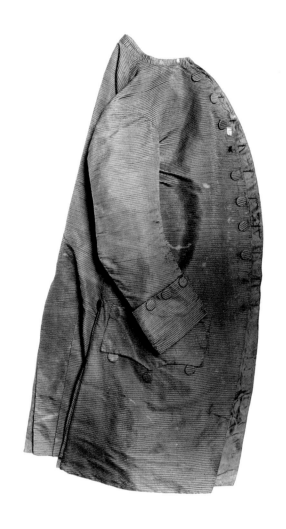

TIME

Benjamin Franklin:
An Illustrated History
of His Life and Times

TIME

MANAGING EDITOR Richard Stengel
ART DIRECTOR D.W. Pine

Benjamin Franklin:
An Illustrated History of His Life and Times

EDITOR/WRITER Richard Lacayo
DESIGNER Sharon Okamoto
PICTURE EDITOR Patricia Cadley
RESEARCHERS Kathleen Adams, Elizabeth Bland
EDITORIAL PRODUCTION Lionel P. Vargas

TIME INC. HOME ENTERTAINMENT
PUBLISHER Richard Fraiman
GENERAL MANAGER Steven Sandonato
EXECUTIVE DIRECTOR, MARKETING SERVICES Carol Pittard
DIRECTOR, RETAIL & SPECIAL SALES Tom Mifsud
DIRECTOR, NEW PRODUCT DEVELOPMENT Peter Harper
DIRECTOR, BOOKAZINE MARKETING Laura Adam
PUBLISHING DIRECTOR, BRAND MARKETING Joy Butts
ASSISTANT GENERAL COUNSEL Helen Wan
BOOK PRODUCTION MANAGER Suzanne Janso
DESIGN & PREPRESS MANAGER Anne-Michelle Gallero
ASSOCIATE BRAND MANAGER Michela Wilde

SPECIAL THANKS TO:

Christine Austin, Jeremy Biloon, Glenn Buonocore, Jim Childs, Susan Chodakiewicz, Rose Cirrincione,
Jacqueline Fitzgerald, Carrie Frazier, Lauren Hall, Jennifer Jacobs, Brynn Joyce, Mona Li, Robert Marasco, Amy Migliaccio,
Richard Prue, Brooke Reger, Dave Rozzelle, Ilene Schreider, Adriana Tierno, Alex Voznesenskiy, Sydney Webber,
Jonathan White, FORTUNE Copy Desk, TIME Imaging

Published by TIME Books, Time Inc.
1271 Avenue of the Americas, New York, N.Y. 10020

ISBN 10: 1-60320-108-4   ISBN 13: 978-1-60320-108-7   Library of Congress Control Number: 2009940852

We welcome your comments and suggestions about Time Books. Please write to us at:
Time Books, Attention: Book Editors, PO Box 11016, Des Moines, Iowa 50336-1016

If you would like to order any of our hardcover Collector's Edition books, please call us at 1-800-327-6388
(Monday through Friday, 7 a.m.–8 p.m. or Saturday, 7 a.m.–6 p.m. central time).

B
1706
BENJAMIN FRANKLIN printer DISTINGUISHED
IN SCIENCE & POLITICS
D
1790

CONTENTS

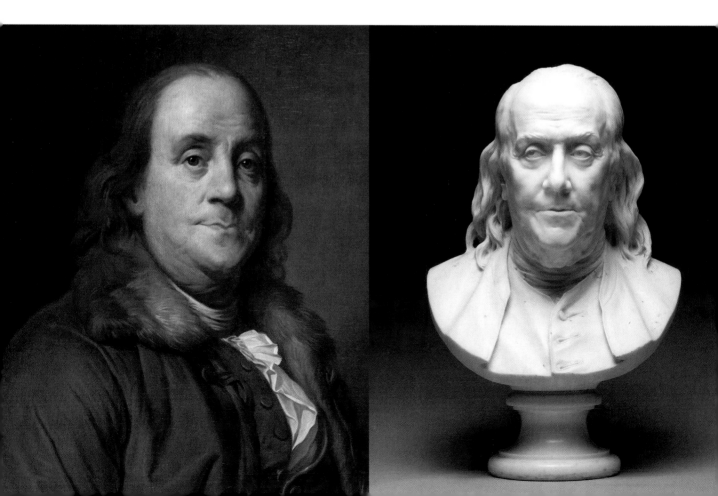

THE FOUNDER WITH A HUMAN FACE

By Richard Lacayo

Of all the founding fathers, Benjamin Franklin may have been the most widely accomplished. His work as a scientist and inventor made him the most famous American of his day, not just in North America but all across Europe. He was the nation's first and perhaps its greatest diplomat, the central figure behind two essential achievements—the alliance with France that was crucial to the American victory in the Revolutionary War and the treaty with Britain that brought that war to a close. He was a political thinker, the architect of designs for representative government, and a political activist, a forceful polemicist, and tireless pamphleteer. As if all that weren't enough, he was a considerable literary figure, the author of an enduring autobiography and father of an endless line of shrewd comic characters, from Silence Dogood to Poor Richard.

Yet among the great early figures of the American republic, Franklin, this perennial overachiever, still seems the most human. Less majestic than George Washington, less cerebral than Thomas Jefferson, more down to earth than John Adams, he can appear at times not so much a founding father as a founding uncle, funny, intimate and easygoing. Though he ended his life as a man who felt at home in the most aristocratic circles of Paris, he remains for us the quintessential American Everyman, born in modest circumstances but possessed of a surplus of energy and ambition and a willingness to work his way up in a new society that made it possible for men of exactly his kind to thrive. In other words, he was the American middle class personified, or at least the embodiment of the qualities the middle class likes to see in itself—practicality, ingenuity, business sense and a confidence that stops short of hubris. He's the tradesman as statesman. And that's one good definition of an ideal American type.

STEALING THUNDER
Benjamin West's portrait of an Olympian Franklin is very unlike our usual image of him.

6

HIS LIFE
AND WORKS

1722
Writes "Silence Dogood" letters

1723
Flees to Philadelphia and takes job as printer's assistant

1706
Born in Boston on Milk Street, Jan. 17

1718
Is apprenticed to his brother James, a printer

1753
Becomes co–deputy postmaster of the colonies

1754
French and Indian War begins; in Albany, proposes plan to join the colonies together

1752
Flies kite with son William in experiment that links lightning to electricity

1775
Elected to the Second Continental Congress; proposes the first Articles of Confederation

1778
Signs treaties of alliance, amity, and commerce with France

1776
Helps draft the Declaration of Independence; sails to France

1782
With John Adams and John Jay, negotiates peace treaty with Britain

1730
Enters common-law marriage with Deborah Read

1732
Publishes the first edition of Poor Richard's Almanack

1736
Forms the Union Fire Company, a volunteer brigade

1737
Is appointed Philadelphia postmaster

1743
Organizes the American Philosophical Society

1749
Proposes academy that becomes the University of Pennsylvania

1751
Co-founds the Pennsylvania Hospital

1762
Invents glass armonica, a musical instrument

1763
End of French and Indian War; makes postal inspection tour through the colonies

1764
Paxton Boys episode; loses Assembly seat; returns to London

1765
Stamp Act passes in the House of Commons

1774
Privy Council hearings, with Franklin questioned in the Cockpit

1783
Witnesses first manned balloon flight

1787
At Constitutional Convention, formally proposes great compromise that creates a House with proportional representation and a Senate with equal number of votes per state

1790
Dies on April 17 at the age of 84

HUMBLE
BEGINNINGS

Benjamin Franklin was born in Boston and became one of the exemplary Americans of his day. But he was descended from a family with a deep attachment to England. By the time his father, Josiah, sailed for Massachusetts in 1683, the Franklins had lived for three centuries in the tiny village of Ecton, in Northamptonshire, an area northwest of London where the family owned a 30-acre farm. The very name Franklin was a sign of their origins. It derived from *frankeleyn*—Middle English for freeman, a social category that emerged in the Middle Ages. These were Englishmen who had money and property but no claim to an aristocratic family line—precursors, you might say, of the entrepreneurial middle classes that Franklin would come to epitomize.

In religion the Franklins had been staunch Protestants from the early days of the Reformation. In his *Autobiography* Franklin relates a bit of family lore from the reign of Queen Mary I. That would be "Bloody Mary," the daughter of Henry VIII who tried to undo her father's break with Rome and restore the Catholic faith throughout her realm. During her five tumultuous years on the throne Protestants were persecuted, and religious authorities were on the lookout for surreptitious heretics. Franklin tells us that his great-great-grandfather Thomas, who was determined to go on reading to his family from the now forbidden English Bible, attached a copy to the underside of a household stool. When he wanted to read Scripture he would turn the stool upside down on his lap. But whenever he did that, Franklin explains, he posted one of his children at the door, "to give notice if he saw the apparitor coming, who was an officer of the spiritual court. In that case the stool was turned down again upon its feet…"

More than a century later it would be another episode of religious persecution, this time of Puritans by the Church of England, that would play a role in the decision by Franklin's father to make what must have been the difficult decision to leave for the colonies.

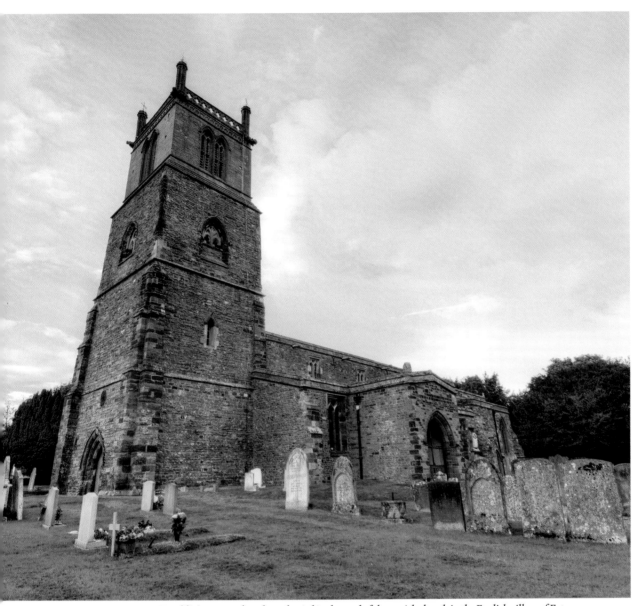

THE ANCESTRAL VILLAGE *Franklin's aunt and uncle are buried in the yard of the parish church in the English village of Ecton.*

LIFE IN THE OLD COUNTRY
In this pair of period woodcuts we see the world of 17th-century England that Franklin's father, Josiah, was born into. Above, a Puritan family gathers at the dinner table. At right, a housewife spins thread outside her cottage while a gentleman and his hounds pursue a fleeing buck.

RELIGIOUS STRIFE

The England of Josiah Franklin's youth was torn by the prolonged struggle between the Church of England and Puritan reformers. At top, a woodcut depicts a dissenting preacher as a "false Prophet." At right, King Charles II, who restored the monarchy and the power of the Church of England after the Puritan revolt. Above, a woodcut from a pro-Puritan tract represents a Puritan minister at left as a man "of God," in contrast to a pair of worldly Anglican clerics.

THE DEPARTURE Seventeenth-century England was a society of hereditary rights, especially in the realm of property. Wealth, land, and businesses were passed on exclusively to the eldest son of each generation. Among the Franklins, for instance, there was a family blacksmith shop. But as his father's fourth son, Josiah Franklin had no claim to any part of it. Compelled to make his own way in the world, in his teens Josiah left Ecton for the nearby town of Banbury, where he apprenticed himself to his older brother John as a cloth dyer. At the age of 19 he also acquired a wife, Anne, who quickly bore three children. But by the time he completed his apprenticeship it was apparent that his brother's shop would not generate enough business to support two families. He would need to find another trade, or another town, or both.

Whatever his financial predicaments, Josiah might well have remained in England all his life had it not been for the religious crisis set off by the Stuart Restoration. In 1649 the Stuart king Charles I was overthrown and executed by the forces of Parliament. That event ushered in more than a decade of Puritan rule, years that Charles's son, who would become Charles II, spent mostly in exile in France and the Netherlands. But in 1660 the younger Charles was invited to return to England, where he reclaimed the throne without bloodshed and restored the Church of England as the official faith.

As a Dissenter—a Protestant who rejected practices of the Church of England that appeared too similar to those of the Church of Rome—Josiah was troubled by the loosening of Puritan doctrine that Charles II initiated and the limits placed on the rights of dissenting congregants. The restrictions on his faith combined with his limited economic prospects prompted him to a difficult decision—to seek a freer and more secure life in the New World.

In 1683 Josiah, Anne, and their three young children boarded a ship bound for Boston.

SETTING UP IN A NEW WORLD As Josiah Franklin would learn soon after his arrival, Boston already had more dyers than it could use. Compelled to learn another trade, eventually he found his way to candle and soap making. It was a harsh occupation—for one thing, the tallow for candles was rendered from stinking animal fat—but one that could provide a good living.

A few years after the Franklins set down in Boston, Anne died after giving birth to their seventh child, who survived. Not five months had gone by before Josiah, now 32, had remarried. His new wife was Abiah Folger, 10 years his junior, a young woman he and Anne had gotten to know at Boston's South Church. Josiah and Abiah would go on to have 10 children together. The eighth, born on Jan. 17, 1706, would be a son they would name after Josiah's older brother—Benjamin.

Benjamin Franklin came into the world in a rented house on Boston's Milk Street. It was a small place—just two rooms for an enormous family. Ben was the 15th of his father's children by his two successive wives, and there

EARLY DAYS
At top, Franklin's birthplace, the rented house on Milk Street. The portrait above is believed to show his mother, Abiah Folger Franklin, in 1707.

would be two more little Franklins to come, both girls. The family would remain in the Milk Street house for the first six years of Franklin's life, until his father was able to buy a larger place at the corner of Union and Hanover Streets. At that house the Franklins were joined for a time by Josiah's brother Benjamin. Arriving from England in 1715, the elder Benjamin spent four years idling around the house writing poetry and collecting sermons, with Josiah all the while growing ever more tired of his presence.

As the years went by young Franklin matured into a broad-shouldered, athletic boy and an avid swimmer at a time when recreational swimming was still an unusual pursuit. In a letter written many years later from France, Franklin provided an enchanting recollection of himself in boyhood. On a summer's day he was flying a kite on the shore of a mill pond when he decided to take a dip and so staked his kite to the ground. Then he opted to retrieve the kite and return to the water, letting it pull him around by wind power while he floated all the way across the pond—"without the least fatigue" as he later recalled, "and with the greatest pleasure imaginable."

It would not be the last time that he would find a way to make the most of a kite.

A Prospect of the Colledges in Cambridge in New England

Franklin's Boston

Founded by Puritan settlers from England in 1630, Boston began as a refuge for religious dissenters. By the year of Franklin's birth, it was also a thriving shipbuilding and seafaring town, the busiest port in England's American colonies, with 1,000 vessels registered with its harbormaster. For many of its people life centered on Boston Harbor and on the Charles River, where the young Franklin would learn his lifelong love of swimming. One of the great features of the waterfront was the Long Wharf, 30 feet wide, which extended a quarter mile into the harbor and was lined with warehouses.

All the same, Boston in the early 18th century was not so much a city as a large town, with a population of around 7,000. By comparison, in those same years London was home to nearly 600,000 people. And though by the 1700s Boston had become a more diverse place, the Puritan influence on local life was still strong. One of the most eminent men in the city was the Calvinist preacher Cotton Mather, who headed the congregation at Boston's Second Church and produced a steady stream of books and pamphlets. Franklin had no use for Puritan orthodoxy. He didn't share Mather's belief in predestination or his conviction that only faith, not good works, mattered to personal salvation. But the Puritan belief that hard work and prosperity were signs of godliness accorded well with Franklin's devotion to industriousness and good business sense, and probably played some role in shaping that attitude.

CITY BY THE SEA

In this map of Boston and its surroundings, published in 1722, you can see the Long Wharf extending into the harbor at center-right. Above it is the Mill Pond that the young Franklin was pulled across one day by a kite he had attached to himself. Above left, Harvard around 1725

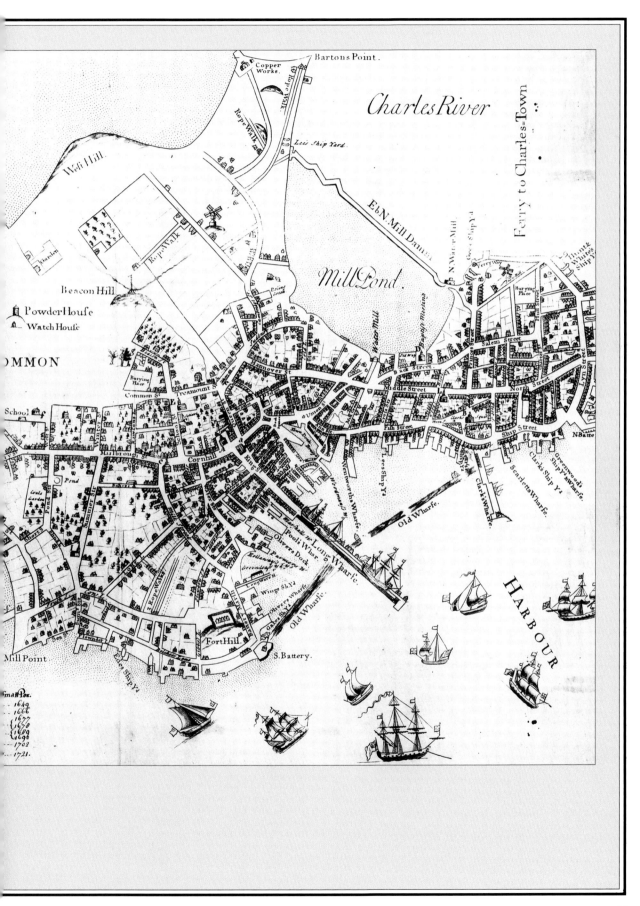

In old age the thrifty Franklin liked to tell friends a story from his boyhood, illustrated here in a 19th-century wood engraving. He recalled having bought a whistle, only to learn from his family that he had paid four times what it was worth. "I cried with vexation," he said, "and the reflection gave me more chagrin than the whistle gave me pleasure."

SCHOOL DAYS Like George Washington and Tom Paine, Franklin had very little formal education. When he was 8 his father sent him for a time to the city's grammar school, which would later become the famed Boston Latin School, in the hope that he would go on to Harvard and eventually become a minister. After less than a year the cost became too much for the family to bear and Josiah pulled his boy out, ending any prospect that Benjamin would enter the gates of Harvard. In later years, that school would be a target of what would be fair to call some envious satire from Franklin.

Afterward Franklin spent a while being tutored in writing and arithmetic by "a then famous man, Mr. George Brownell, very successful in his profession generally," as he put it in the *Autobiography*. He did well in writing but badly in arithmetic, and that second experiment in learning was also brought to a close. With that, at age 10, his formal education was over. Very soon he was drawn back into his father's candle-making business. As he later recalled, he spent his time "cutting wick for the candles, filling the dipping mold and the molds for cast candles, attending the shop, going of errands, etc."

But for a boy with his endless curiosity and intellectual gifts, the life of a chandler would almost certainly have proved too confining. Though no longer in a classroom, the precocious Franklin was dedicated to book learning. As he later wrote: "I do not remember when I could not read."

> "From a child I was fond of reading; and all the little money that came into my hands was ever laid out in books."
>
> — Benjamin Franklin, *Autobiography*

CANDLE MAKER *For a while Franklin worked in his father's shop.*

FINDING THE RIGHT TRADE By the time he was 12, Franklin was restless enough in his father's shop that he began to entertain thoughts of going to sea, if only as a way to escape the monotony of cutting wicks and filling the dipping molds. A life aboard ship was a natural ambition for a boy growing up in a seaport town like Boston. It was also a prospect that horrified his father. Before Franklin's birth, Josiah's firstborn son, also named Josiah, had shipped out on a trading vessel and was never heard from again. Years later the elder Josiah learned that his boy's ship had been lost at sea. To discourage his youngest son from pursuing the same dangerous calling, his father brought him around the city to observe other occupations in the hope he might find one that appealed to him.

It was a search that led eventually to the door of Franklin's elder brother James. He had recently returned from London, where he had learned to become a printer. Once back in Boston, the 21-year-old James had established his own print shop. Despite its connection with books, printing was not the most highly esteemed of occupations. It was hard physical labor that involved carting heavy trays of lead type about the shop, pounding the type into place with wooden mallets, and operating a manual press.

But for men who were energetic and economical—and Franklin would prove to be both of those—there was money to be made. Because the Protestant faithful were expected to read Scripture, literacy in colonial America was widespread, especially among males. The demand for books, sermons, pamphlets, and the fledgling format of newspapers was strong. Franklin signed on to a nine-year apprenticeship under his brother. Ben had some hesitations about the length of the agreement, but as he soon realized, printing—and the access it provided to the world of books he was already discovering—was a trade that would suit him perfectly.

THE BUDDING WRITER Franklin wasn't in the print shop long before he learned that he could not only set type for others, he could also write and publish his own work. In 18th-century America there was a brisk market for poems turned out quickly in response to some notable recent event. James set his bookish younger brother to try his hand at the form. The first of Franklin's attempts, "The Lighthouse Tragedy," was about the drowning of a sea captain and his daughters. The second was a dramatic account of the death of the pirate Edward Teach, better known as Blackbeard. Though Franklin would admit years later that neither poem was any good, the first sold well, which as he later recalled "flattered my vanity." But his father was scornful of the rhyming trade, "telling me verse-makers were generally beggars." So Franklin put aside any thought of a career in balladry.

Besides, he had taken an interest in a more respectable kind of writing. Even before he entered the printers' shops, Franklin's hunger for books had awakened. Though barely an adolescent, he had read John Bunyan's *The Pilgrim's Progress*, Plutarch's *Lives*, and essays by Daniel Defoe and the Pu-

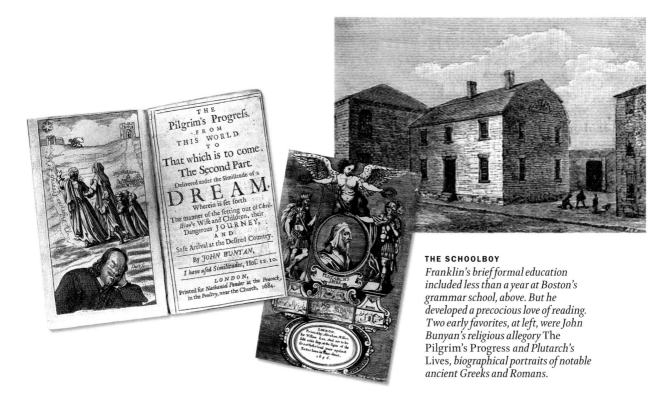

THE SCHOOLBOY
Franklin's brief formal education included less than a year at Boston's grammar school, above. But he developed a precocious love of reading. Two early favorites, at left, were John Bunyan's religious allegory The Pilgrim's Progress *and Plutarch's* Lives, *biographical portraits of notable ancient Greeks and Romans.*

ritan divine Cotton Mather. "From a child I was fond of reading," he wrote later, "and all the little money that came into my hands was ever laid out in books." But with the start of his apprenticeship, as he put it, "I now had access to better books." Now he could also befriend booksellers' apprentices and borrow some of their stock, "which I was careful to return soon and clean."

It was around this time that Franklin discovered *The Spectator*, the London journal that had been founded in 1711 by Joseph Addison and Richard Steele. Their clever, pungent essays filled its pages regularly and made their paper a model of sophisticated journalism for an age that valued pointed wordplay. As they explained to their readers, their purpose as writers was "to enliven morality with wit, and to temper wit with morality…to bring philosophy out of the closets and libraries, schools and colleges, to dwell in clubs and assemblies, at tea-tables and coffeehouses."

It was a formula perfectly suited to Franklin, who had already developed a love of both learning and its practical applications. He devised elaborate exercises to help him learn to write as vividly and persuasively as *The Spectator* wits. He would read one of their essays, take notes on its main points, put it aside for a few days, then try to re-create it from his brief outline. He would render an essay into verse and then back into prose. As a way of learning how to build an argument he would even copy the main points of an essay on separate sheets, scramble them, then try to restore them to the original order. In the *Autobiography* he looks back on all this in a passage of the exquisitely balanced humility and pridefulness that could be so typical of him.

"By comparing my work afterwards with the original I discovered many faults and amended them; but I sometimes had the pleasure of fancying that, in certain particulars of small import, I had been lucky enough to improve the method or the language, and this encouraged me to think I might possibly in time come to be a tolerable English writer, of which I was extremely ambitious."

THE APPRENTICE
After Franklin balked at becoming a candle maker, he entered his brother's print shop, as pictured here in a 19th-century colored engraving.

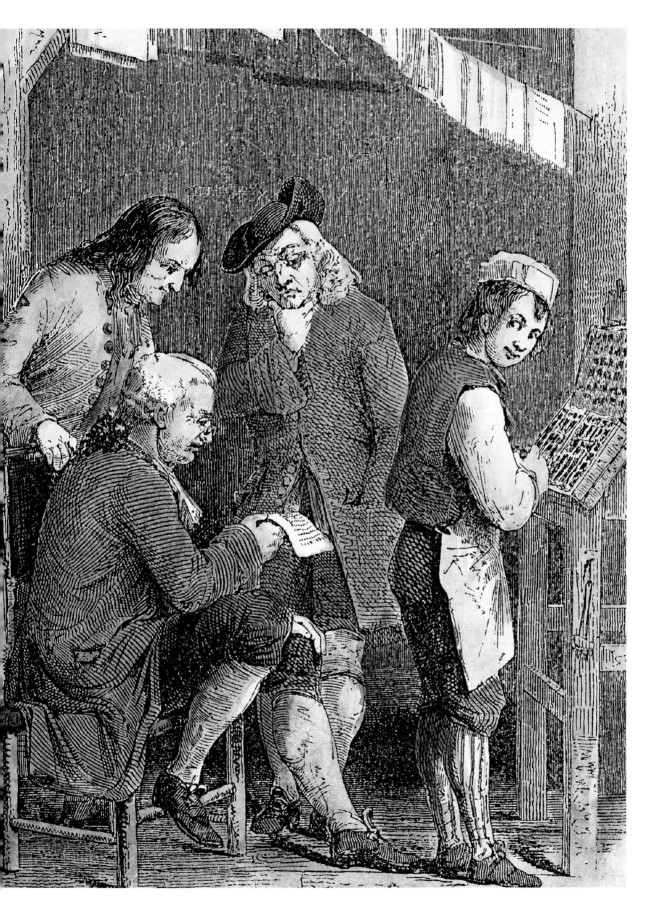

THE PRINTER

The image at right, from an early-20th-century mural, is an artist's imagining of Ben Franklin in what was for decades his natural habitat—a print shop. Printing was the perfect occupation for a man of Franklin's gifts and ambitions. It provided him not only with a good living but also with the opportunity to publish his own newspaper, as well as *Poor Richard's Almanack*.

In Franklin's day, printing was still very much a manual occupation. Printers—there were usually several in each shop—set cast-metal letters into rows and "framed" those rows into pages, typically four per frame. Then they inked the type, laid paper over it, and used a manual press to push the paper against the inked letters. Finally they hung the sheets to dry and later cut and, if necessary, bound them.

TOOLS OF THE TRADE
Clockwise from top left: The adjustable type gauge measured type to determine the right fit. The ink-stone table held printer's ink. Leather balls were used to dab the ink onto the type. The spoon was for pouring molten type metal. The composing stick (opposite page) held lines of type as they were transferred to galleys.

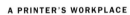

HIS PERSONAL LETTERS

These type matrices—molds for producing type from molten metal—were owned by Franklin and used by him in his press at the estate in Passy outside Paris, where he lived during his years in France.

A PRINTER'S WORKPLACE

At Franklin Court in Philadelphia, a collection of museums and exhibition spaces on the site where Franklin's home once stood, visitors can see this re-creation of an 18th-century print shop like the one he owned. It includes a flatbed printing press, seen here with framed type ready to be inked.

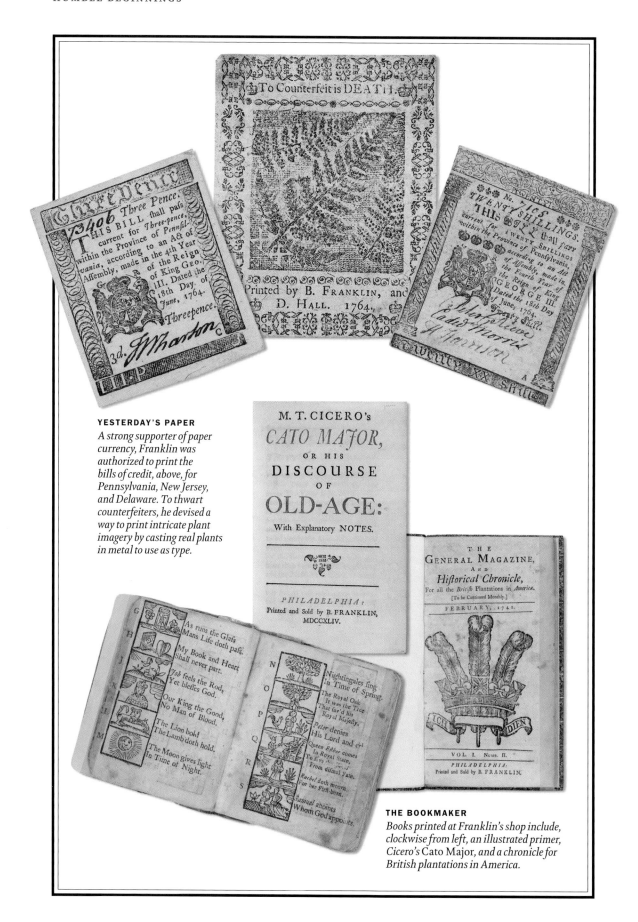

YESTERDAY'S PAPER

A strong supporter of paper currency, Franklin was authorized to print the bills of credit, above, for Pennsylvania, New Jersey, and Delaware. To thwart counterfeiters, he devised a way to print intricate plant imagery by casting real plants in metal to use as type.

THE BOOKMAKER

Books printed at Franklin's shop include, clockwise from left, an illustrated primer, Cicero's Cato Major, and a chronicle for British plantations in America.

"Teach and Maynard on the quarter,
Fought it out most manfully;
Maynard's sword did cut him shorter,
Losing his head he there did die."

— BENJAMIN FRANKLIN, *from his ballad about
the death of the pirate Edward Teach, better known as Blackbeard*

HE THAT HATH
A TRADE
HATH AN ESTATE.

THE SOUND OF YOUR
HAMMER AT FIVE
IN THE MORNING OR
AT NINE AT NIGHT
HEARD BY A CREDITOR
MAKES HIM EASY
SIX MONTHS LONGER.

WHEN MEN ARE
EMPLOYED THEY ARE
BEST CONTENTED.

VERSES FOR SALE *An old postcard shows Franklin peddling his ballads. The proverbs are from other Franklin writings.*

THE COURANT In 1721 Franklin's brother James decided to start a newspaper. At the time Boston had only two papers. One, the *Boston News-Letter*, was published by John Campbell, a printer who was also Boston's former postmaster. The other, the *Boston Gazette*, was published by Campbell's successor as postmaster, William Brooker. For a time the *Gazette* had been printed by Franklin's brother, until he lost the contract and decided to start a paper of his own. Franklin later recalled that some of his brother's friends tried to discourage James—"one newspaper being, in their judgment, enough for America."

As postmaster, Brooker had a ready-made distribution network for his paper over the postal routes he controlled. Since he occupied an official post, he could also claim that his *Gazette* was a government authorized publication. This might seem a strange thing for a newspaper to treat as a boast, but at a time when government had the power to shutter an offending publication, it seemed natural, or at least prudent, for a paper to want the mantle of officialdom. Early newspapers also depended on printing contracts from government, so publishers tried to stay on the good side of the authorities.

But James Franklin's paper, the *New-England Courant*, would be a different animal, truly independent and even feisty, entirely willing to pick fights with the local establishment and power elites. Franklin tells us that his brother's paper also raised the bar of journalistic quality by including well-written contributions by some of James's more "ingenious" friends. And very soon the ranks of ingenious *Courant* writers would include an audacious newcomer—Benjamin Franklin.

ENTER SILENCE DOGOOD Franklin made his first appearance in a newspaper in a very unusual way—in the guise of a country widow, author of a series of witty, moralizing letters to readers that were published under the name "Silence Dogood." Franklin quietly slipped the first of them under the door of his brother's print shop one night. Not knowing who had written the letter but delighted by its homespun humor and wisdom, James published it in the *Courant* on April 2, 1722. "I am courteous and affable," is how Dogood introduced herself to the world, "good humored (unless I am first provoked) and handsome, and sometimes witty."

In many of her letters Dogood pokes gentle fun at New England habits and institutions, as when she proposes a "recipe" for a New England funeral elegy. "Take one of your neighbors who has lately departed this life," she advises. "It will be best if he went away suddenly, *being killed, drowned or froze to death.*" But the opinionated Dogood could also be deadly earnest, as when she tells us that she is "naturally very jealous for the rights and liberties of my country; and the least appearance of an encroachment on those invaluable privileges, is apt to make my blood boil exceedingly. I have likewise a natural inclination to observe and reprove the faults of others, at which I have an excellent faculty." And in one of them she takes the opportunity to lampoon Harvard, the college Franklin never entered because of his father's decision to end his formal schooling. Dogood describes for readers a dream in which she witnessed the vices of an institution where the students learned "little more than how to carry themselves handsomely, and enter a room genteelly, (which might as well be acquired at a dancing-school,) and from thence they return, after abundance of trouble and charge, as great blockheads as ever, only more proud and self-conceited."

In all there would be 14 Dogood letters, the last of them appearing in October, by which time Franklin's brother had begun to suspect their true authorship. Franklin tells us that James wasn't pleased to realize that his younger sibling had written these much praised essays, as "he thought, probably with reason, that it tended to make me too vain."

THE STARTING POINT
It was in this issue of his brother James's newspaper that Franklin published the first of the wry letters he wrote under the pen name Silence Dogood.

FAREWELL TO BOSTON In the summer of 1722, while the *Courant* was publishing the Dogood letters, the Massachusetts General Court summarily jailed James Franklin. His offense was to have insulted the colonial authorities by publishing an anonymous letter in his paper—written, of course, by him—that mocked their poor efforts to pursue coastal pirates. For two heady weeks, while his brother languished in jail, the 16-year-old Franklin stepped in as acting publisher and editor.

As he tells us in his *Autobiography*: "I had the management of the paper, and I made bold to give our rulers some rubs in it, which my brother took very kindly, while others began to consider me in an unfavorable light as a young genius that had a turn for libeling and satire."

By year's end James was in trouble again, this time for publishing an attack on religion. Now the authorities demanded he submit every issue of the *Courant* for their advance approval. Instead James fled, taking care first to arrange for his brother to publish the *Courant*. To make it appear that Benjamin was independent of his brother he also released him from his indenture. But at the same time he forced Ben to sign a secret agreement pledging to continue as James's apprentice for another three years. "A very flimsy scheme it was," Franklin tells us.

For several months thereafter, the *Courant* appeared with Franklin as its nominal publisher. But all the while his relations with his brother were deteriorating, especially because James had taken to beating him. But Franklin saw a way out. He suspected James would never attempt to enforce the secret apprenticeship agreement, which would require him to admit that he had tried to deceive the General Court.

So Franklin decided to skip town. He quietly boarded ship for New York. Three days later he was there, "near 300 miles from home, a boy of but 17, without the least recommendations to, or knowledge of any person in the place, and with very little money in my pocket." ■

SIBLING RIVALRY *A 19th-century engraving of Franklin being mistreated by his brother*

SETTING OUT
IN THE WORLD

An East Perspective View of the **CITY** *of* **PHILADELPHIA**, *in the PRO...*

1. Christ Church 3. Academy 5. Dutch Calvinist Church 7. Quaker Meeting
2. State House 4. Presbyterian Church 6. The Court House 8. High Street Whar...

ngraved from the Original Drawing sent over from
hiladelphia, in the possession of Carington Bowles.

Printed for and Sold by **CARINGTON BOWLES**, at his Map &Print War...

HOME BASE *Though he would live for many years in England and France, Franklin would always return to Philadelphia.*

26

Franklin stopped off just briefly in New York. There the town's only printer, William Bradford, advised him to continue on to Philadelphia, where Bradford's son Andrew, also a printer, had just lost his principal assistant. After a difficult six-day journey by water around the coast of New Jersey and a final trek by foot, Franklin made his entry into the city where so much of his destiny would be played out.

In the *Autobiography* Franklin leaves us a memorable picture of his arrival in Philadelphia in October 1723, dirty from his hard journey and in workman's dress because his better clothing had not yet arrived by boat. After stopping at a baker to buy three rolls, he tells us he proceeded up Market Street, in the process passing the house of a carpenter, John Read, whose daughter Deborah would someday become Franklin's common-law wife. As it happened, Deborah was standing in the doorway of her father's house as Franklin walked by, and he tells us that she "thought I made, as I certainly did, a most awkward, ridiculous appearance."

CE of PENSYLVANIA, in NORTH AMERICA: *taken from the JERSEY Shore.*

9 . Mulberry Street	11 . Vine Street	13 . Draw Bridge	The other Streets are not to be
10 . Saßafras Street	12 . Chesnut Street	14 . Corn Mill	seen from the point of Sight . —

Nº 69 in S.t Pauls Church Yard. LONDON. Publish'd as the Act directs, 1 Jan.e 1778.

NEW BOY *In his* Autobiography *Franklin describes how, on his first day in Philadelphia, his future wife spied him from a doorway.*

Franklin set about quickly to get himself established. Though Andrew Bradford didn't have enough work to take him on, Bradford introduced him to a rival printer, Samuel Keimer, who offered him a job. Through Keimer, Franklin found lodging with John Read, which made it a simple matter to court Read's 15-year-old daughter. He was by that year a well-built young man of more than average height, with an upper body made strong by years of swimming and hauling heavy trays of lead type around print shops. Deborah apparently took notice.

Soon Franklin made another fateful acquaintance. His brother-in-law, Robert Holmes, was the captain of a sloop that traded along the coast between Boston and Delaware. Having learned that Franklin had fled to Philadelphia, Holmes wrote urging that he return to Boston. Franklin sent a reply setting out his reasons for leaving, a letter that Holmes happened to show to a distinguished acquaintance—Sir William Keith, the provincial governor of Pennsylvania.

Keith was impressed that such sophisticated writing was the product of a boy who was not yet 18. As it happened, the provincial government of Pennsylvania provided substantial print business to both Bradford and Keimer, but Keith was unhappy with the quality of their work. Perhaps this precocious boy could be developed into a more qualified tradesman. So he sought Franklin out and proposed that he persuade his father to stake him in business, on the assurance that the governor would provide him a steady stream of orders. Thus inspired, Franklin went home for a while to Boston, but he was unable to persuade his father and soon returned to Philadelphia. At that point Keith made him an even more remarkable offer—that he would bankroll Franklin himself, and that the boy should head at once to London to procure a printing press, type, and other supplies.

Franklin was soon aboard a ship to England, with dreams of a great future in his head.

THE FALSE BENEFACTOR *Sir William Keith, Pennsylvania's governor, seeks out Franklin at Samuel Keimer's print shop.*

HIS FIRST STAY IN LONDON Before he left Philadelphia, Franklin proposed marriage to Deborah Read. But Read's mother, by then a widow, insisted that a wedding should wait until Franklin had returned from abroad—"when I should be, as I expected, set up in my business." But as he boarded the ship bound for London in November 1724, Franklin still had not received the letter of credit for 100 English pounds that Gov. Keith had promised to cover the cost of his purchases in London. All the same he was assured it would be brought onboard before the ship sailed, and he still believed he had no reason to doubt Keith's word.

He was wrong. When he arrived in London on Christmas Eve, Franklin learned there was no such letter. He brought this astonishing news to Thomas Denham, a Quaker merchant who had befriended Franklin during the voyage and who knew the governor as well. As Franklin recalls ruefully in his *Autobiography*, Denham opened a window for him into the governor's character. "[He] told me there was not the least probability that [Keith] had written any letters for me; that no one, who knew him, had the smallest dependence on him; and he laughed at the notion of the governor's giving me a letter of credit, having, as he said, no credit to give."

Having no money for a return passage, Franklin now had to fend for himself in a strange city, though not alone. He had come to London with a friend from Philadelphia, James Ralph, a would-be poet fleeing an unhappy marriage. They rented cheap rooms together, though since Ralph remained unemployed their expenses were covered by Franklin, who soon found work at a large printing house called Palmer's.

It was while working at Palmer's that Franklin published a long philosophical pamphlet, his first. *A Dissertation on Liberty and Necessity, Pleasure and Pain* was the attempt of a thoughtful 19-year-old to come to grips with the contradiction between an all-powerful God and man's capacity for free choice.

BRIGHT LIGHTS, BIG CITY
London was a much larger, more complex and worldly place than Boston or Philadelphia. At right, a map shows the sprawling city in 1724, the year of Franklin's arrival. For a vigorous young man like Franklin, it also offered many temptations like the ones pictured above in a painting from William Hogarth's famous series, A Rake's Progress.

BIG THINKER
In his Dissertation *Franklin made a strenuous youthful foray into theology.*

He managed to conclude that since God is all-powerful, nothing happens without his consent, and that since he is also "all-wise" and "all-good," evil does not exist. To sustain that idea required him to conclude as well that pain and suffering did not exist either, and so were misperceptions. Along the way he also decided that the soul was not immortal. At death, it died too, or perhaps attached itself to a new body, but with no recollection of its previous incarnation.

In later life Franklin would decide that publishing the *Dissertation* had been a mistake, and he burned as many of the 100 printed copies as he could track down. Flawed though it may have been as an intellectual exercise, it was an early instance of his lifelong attempt to establish for himself a working definition of God, no matter how far it departed from the conventional Christian understanding, and of his indifference to the Calvinist dogmas that had surrounded him in Boston.

It's hard not to wonder whether Franklin may have been led to compose an argument against the existence of evil in part because he was feeling guilty about sexual temptations he had succumbed to in London. In the *Autobiography* Franklin describes the habit of "intrigues with low women" that

he fell into occasionally as a young man, "which were attended with some expense and great inconvenience, besides a continual risk to my health." His friendship with James Ralph, the aspiring poet, also ended when Franklin tried—without success—to seduce Ralph's girlfriend while Ralph was away from London. Meanwhile, during his 18 months in England, Franklin managed to write just once to his presumed fiancée, Deborah Read, and then merely to tell her he would not be home anytime soon.

And in truth, at least for a while, Franklin found London a very agreeable place. His skills as a printer helped him to advance in his work, and he moved from Palmer's to a better-paying job at a larger printer, John Watts. He attended the theaters, made the acquaintance of a few notable men, impressed people with his skills as a swimmer. But then an opportunity presented itself for him to return home. Thomas Denham, the Quaker merchant he had met on the voyage over, decided to return to Philadelphia and open a general store. He offered Franklin passage back across the Atlantic and a job as his shop clerk, with the promise of promotions as the young man learned the business. The 50-pound salary he offered was less than Franklin was making in London, but as he tells us in the *Autobiography*, "I was grown tired of London, remembered with pleasure the happy months I had spent in Pennsylvania, and wish'd again to see it."

On July 23, 1726, he set sail back to America.

WILLIAM PENN

Franklin's Philadelphia

Philadelphia was the first planned city in America, summoned up by William Penn, the Quaker founder of Pennsylvania. After acquiring Pennsylvania as a land grant from Charles II in 1681, Penn directed that a settlement should be built on the western bank of the Delaware River with wide boulevards on a grid pattern and large building lots to keep homes and businesses widely spaced. By the time Franklin arrived in 1723, the city contained about 6,000 people and would soon overtake Boston as the largest among the colonies.

Though 1720s Philadelphia was home to large numbers of non-Quaker immigrants, mainly Germans and Scotch-Irish, the Quakers were still the predominant local influence. Like the Puritans of Boston, they were thrifty and hard working. Unlike the Puritans, they were tolerant of other religious sects. This was, after all, Philadelphia—derived from the Greek for City of Brotherly Love. That tolerance was a quality that the resolutely undoctrinaire Franklin would greatly admire.

Penn had also taken pains to cultivate good relations with the local Indians, so the inhabitants of Philadelphia enjoyed generally friendly dealings with the tribes. Unlike other colonial cities, Philadelphia saw no need for walls or fortifications.

HALLOWED GROUNDS
The Pennsylvania State House, begun in 1732 and completed 21 years later, was in its time the most ambitious civic building in the colonies. We know it now as Independence Hall, where the Declaration of Independence would be adopted in 1776 and the Constitution in 1789. Franklin helped to produce both.

RETURN TO PHILADELPHIA Franklin may have lived a mildly dissolute life in London, but on the voyage home he resolved that in the future he would conduct himself more prudently. To that end, while still at sea he drew up a set of personal guidelines, the first of several he would produce throughout a life much given to self-inspection and codes of virtue. His "Plan of Conduct" is worth reproducing in full for the picture it offers of a very earnest young man:

> It is necessary for me to be extremely frugal for some time, till I have paid what I owe.
>
> To endeavour to speak truth in every instance; to give nobody expectations that are not likely to be answered, but aim at sincerity in every word and action—the most amiable excellence in a rational being.
>
> To apply myself industriously to whatever business I take in hand, and not divert my mind from my business by any foolish project of growing suddenly rich; for industry and patience are the surest means of plenty.
>
> I resolve to speak ill of no man whatever, not even in a matter of truth; but rather by some means excuse the faults I hear charged upon others, and upon proper occasions speak all the good I know of every body.

In his first months back in Philadelphia, Franklin settled into his new occupation as salesman in Denham's shop. He roomed with Denham and came to think of him as a father figure. "I respected and loved him," he tells us. But within a few months Denham took ill and died. "He left me a small legacy," Franklin wrote. "And he left me once more to the wide world."

SOCIABLE MAN *An engraving from 1848 pictures Franklin, right, with members of his Junto.*

HIS HOT TOPICS

Franklin drew up a list of 24 subjects the members of the Junto, his social networking group, might talk about each week. Here are some:

1. *Have you met with anything in the author you last read remarkable or suitable to be communicated to the Junto?*

3. *Hath any citizen in your knowledge failed in his business lately; and what have you heard of the cause?*

4. *Have you lately heard of any citizen's thriving well, and by what means?*

5. *Have you lately heard how any present rich man, here or elsewhere, got his estate?*

6. *Do you know of any fellow citizen who has lately done a worthy action deserving praise and imitation? Or who has committed an error proper for us to be warned against and avoid?*

7. *What unhappy effects of intemperance have you lately observed or heard? Of imprudence? Of passion? Or of any other vice or folly?*

8. *What happy effects of temperance? Of prudence? Of moderation? Or of any other virtue?*

14. *Have you lately observed any defect in the laws of your country for which it would be proper to move the legislature for an amendment...?*

15. *Have you lately observed any encroachments on the just liberties of the people?*

16. *Hath anybody attacked your reputation lately, and what can the Junto do toward securing it?*

17. *Is there any man whose friendship you want and which the Junto or any of them can procure for you?*

20. *In what manner can the Junto or any of them assist you in any of your honorable designs?*

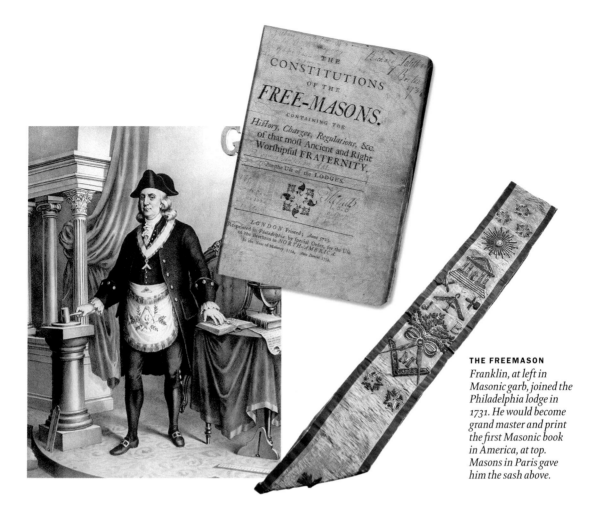

THE FREEMASON
Franklin, at left in Masonic garb, joined the Philadelphia lodge in 1731. He would become grand master and print the first Masonic book in America, at top. Masons in Paris gave him the sash above.

With few other prospects, Franklin accepted an offer from his old employer, Samuel Keimer, to return to Keimer's print shop, this time as manager. But it would be a short-lived association. Franklin suspected that Keimer had brought him aboard at a relatively generous wage only to train his four low-paid and unskilled apprentices, with a plan to let him go once they were capable of doing the job on their own. Keimer was a disagreeable man at best, an "odd fish" Franklin called him, and a man who was "slovenly to extreme dirtiness." Eventually they argued, and Franklin walked out.

Before long he would be persuaded to return, but this time he had a secret exit strategy. One of the Keimer apprentices, Hugh Meredith, had proposed that he and Franklin become partners in a new shop that Meredith's father would bankroll. But first Meredith would have to complete his term of apprenticeship.

In the meantime Franklin helped Keimer to complete an important commission, a new issue of paper currency ordered by the New Jersey Assembly. Because paper money was easily counterfeited, Franklin devised the first copperplate press in America, a process he had learned about in England. On the soft copper Franklin was able to engrave an elaborate design that would be almost impossible for counterfeiters to copy. The currency job also brought Franklin into the company of notables from the New Jersey colonial government, who invited him into their homes and found his company much more agreeable than they did the "knavish" and dirty Keimer.

Soon after that job was complete, Franklin and Meredith went into business for themselves. In short order customers began arriving, but so did problems. As an apprentice at Keimer's, Meredith had been fond of drink. Franklin had persuaded him for a time to stay sober, but he soon lapsed back into his old habits and became a burden and an embarrassment. Franklin eventually found new backers who helped him to buy out his partner's share of the business. Meredith decamped to North Carolina to return to farming. At the age of 23, Franklin was now truly his own man.

NEXT OF KIN
Franklin had a fond but often distant relationship with his common-law wife, Deborah, seen at left in a portrait that once hung in their Philadelphia home. Their son Francis, whom they called Franky, was just 4 when he died of smallpox. The portrait above was done as a memorial after his death in 1736.

THE JUNTO AND FREEMASONRY Franklin was a sole proprietor now but by no means an isolated one. Even onboard the ship that brought him back to Philadelphia he had confided to his journal the reflection that "man is a sociable being and it is, for aught I know, one of the worst punishments to be excluded from society."

Certainly Franklin was a sociable being, and very soon after he had settled himself back in the city, in the fall of 1727, he formed a sort of fraternal organization of tradesmen and craftsmen called the Junto. Part drinking club, part debating society, part mutual assistance network, it consisted of about a dozen young men who met every Friday evening, first at a tavern but later in a room they rented for the purpose. Members discussed topics in morals, politics, or natural philosophy. Franklin directed that their debates were "to be conducted in the sincere spirit of inquiry after truth, without fondness for dispute, or desire of victory." Members who broke the rules of amicable discussion were subject to fines.

The French writer Alexis de Tocqueville, during his famous tour of America in 1831, would observe that a defining characteristic of Americans was the tendency to form themselves into voluntary associations. A century before de Tocqueville's travels, Franklin's Junto was just that, a fraternity of entrepreneurs and working men who were dedicated to self-improvement, the performance of good works, and social networking. With one exception, "a young gentleman of some fortune," the first members of the Junto came entirely from the middling stations of Philadelphia society—a copier of deeds, a surveyor, a shoemaker and four printers or printers' apprentices, including Franklin.

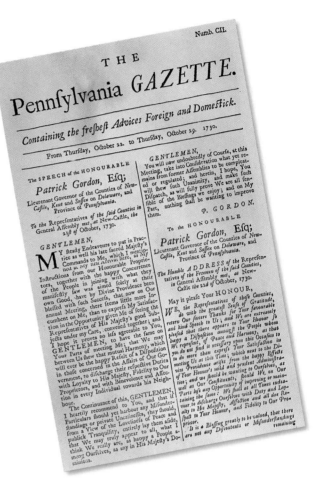

These were men of America's emerging middle class—or men who aspired to that standing—the social category that Franklin would come to symbolize to the world.

In 1731 Franklin would also join an already existing fraternal organization—the Freemasons. In 18th-century America, membership in the Masons made it possible for tradesmen and artisans to rub shoulders with gentlemen of greater wealth and social standing. The Masonic dedication to good works and religious tolerance ideally suited Franklin, and in time he would become grand master of Pennsylvania. So much the better that his fellow Masons also sent work his way, including the job of printing *The Constitutions of the Free-Masons*, the first Masonic book published in America.

THE GAZETTE AND MARRIAGE—OF A SORT Though Franklin was proud to be a printer, he increasingly regarded himself as a writer as well as a thinker and commentator. For some time Franklin had been musing about putting out a newspaper, as his brother had done in Boston. Philadelphia already had one, the *American Weekly Mercury*, published by the city's other printer, Andrew Bradford, but Franklin didn't think much of it. "A paltry thing," he called it, "wretchedly managed, and in no way entertaining."

Unfortunately he mentioned his plans to George Webb, an apprentice in Keimer's shop. Webb conveyed the news to Keimer, who decided to get the jump on Franklin by abruptly starting a paper of his own with the tongue-tying name the *Universal Instructor in All Arts and Sciences; and Pennsylvania Gazette*. This led Franklin to an ingenious revenge.

It happened that to fill his paper Keimer was reprinting articles from an encyclopedia, working in alphabetical order. His first installment happened to include an entry on abortion. That gave Franklin his opportunity. He supplied Bradford's paper with what were supposed to be letters from ordinary readers attacking Keimer's paper. They were of course by Franklin, and like the Silence Dogood letters, written under false names. One was "Martha Careful," who warned Keimer that "if he proceed farther to expose the secrets of our sex in that audacious manner...my sister Molly and myself, with some others, are resolved to run the hazard of taking him by the beard, at the next place we meet him, and make an example of him for his immodesty."

Franklin would provide further letters to Bradford's paper under the pen name "The Busy-Body," some lampooning Keimer, some mocking human foibles generally. Eventually he would buy out Keimer, who sailed off to Barbados. On Oct. 2, 1729, Franklin published his first issue of the paper he now called simply the *Pennsylvania Gazette*.

God helps them that help themselves.

Where there's marriage without love, there will be love without marriage.

Early to bed and early to rise, makes a man healthy, wealthy and wise.

Love your enemies, for they will tell you your faults.

Three may keep a secret if two of them are dead.

— BENJAMIN FRANKLIN,
from Poor Richard's Almanack

Poor Richard, 1733.

AN

Almanack

For the Year of Chrift

1 7 3 3,

Being the Firft after LEAP YEAR:

And makes fince the Creation   Years

By the Account of the Eaftern Greeks   7241

By the Latin Church, when ☉ ent. ♈   6932

By the Computation of *W.W.*   5742

By the Roman Chronology   5682

By the *Jewifh* Rabbies   5494

Wherein is contained

The Lunations, Eclipfes, Judgment of the Weather, Spring Tides, Planets Motions & mutual Afpects, Sun and Moon's Rifing and Setting, Length of Days, Time of High Water, Fairs, Courts, and obfervable Days.

Fitted to the Latitude of Forty Degrees, and a Meridian of Five Hours Weft from *London,* but may without fenfible Error, ferve all the adjacent Places, even from *Newfoundland* to South-

---

One year later Franklin would also marry—in a way. During his stay in London he had all but forgotten Deborah Read, who consoled herself by marrying a potter named John Rogers. But soon she was hearing rumors that Rogers already had a wife he had abandoned in England. He also began running up debts. An exasperated Deborah left him and moved back in with her mother. Soon after, Rogers ran off to the West Indies. This left Deborah in a legal limbo. Pennsylvania law didn't recognize desertion as grounds for divorce. The situation became more complicated when rumors reached Philadelphia that Rogers had died. But with no proof of his death, Deborah might have to wait years before the law would recognize her as a widow who could marry again.

On his return from London, though he was in the market for a wife, Franklin didn't beat a path to Deborah's door. He looked first for a woman who might come with a considerable dowry. Only after he failed in that quest did he renew his courtship of his old flame. Deborah and her mother welcomed his attentions as a way out of her own difficulties. But the possibility that her first husband might still be alive made marriage a tricky proposition. Bigamy was a crime punishable for both parties by 39 lashes and life in prison. So the pair settled on an expedient that was not that unusual in the American colonies—common-law marriage. In September 1730 they simply moved in together. They would never formally wed.

And there would be another unorthodox element of their household. Within a few months Franklin brought home an infant he had fathered by another woman. In his *Autobiography* Franklin does not name the mother. But he assumed sole custody of the child, a son he called William. He adored the boy, who would ultimately play a heartbreaking role in his life. On Oct. 20, 1732, Deborah made her own contribution to the household with the birth of a son, Francis.

They may not have made what some people think of as a traditional family, but they were a family all the same.

Above the image, the following captions appear within the illustrations:

WANT OF CARE DOES US MORE DAMAGE THAN WANT OF KNOWLEDGE.

HE WHO SAVES NOT AS HE GETS, MAY KEEP HIS NOSE ALL HIS LIFE TO THE GRINDSTONE, AND DIE NOT WORTH A GROAT.

WANT OF A NAIL THE SHOE WAS LOST, AND FOR WANT OF A SHOE THE HORSE WAS LOST.

A FAT KITCHEN MAKES A LEAN WILL. WOULD YOU BE RICH THINK OF SAVING.

WHAT THOU HAST NO NEED OF, AND ERE LONG THOU WILT SELL THY NECESSARIES.

SILKS AND SATINS, SCARLET AND VELVETS, PUT OUT THE KITCHEN FIRE.

A GREAT PENNYWORTH PAUSE AWHILE. MANY ARE RUINED BY BUYING BARGAINS.

ALWAYS TAKING OUT OF THE MEAL TUB AND NEVER PUTTING IN, SOON COMES TO THE BOTTOM.

HIS MORAL PERFECTION PROJECT

In his Autobiography *Franklin tells us—with tongue slightly in cheek—that around 1728 he conceived "the bold and arduous project of arriving at moral perfection." That required him first to identify 13 virtues. Above, a 19th-century print illustrates lessons from* Poor Richard's Almanack.

1. TEMPERANCE
Eat not to dullness. Drink not to elevation.

2. SILENCE
Speak not but what may benefit others or yourself. Avoid trifling conversation.

3. ORDER
Let all your things have their places. Let each part of your business have its time.

4. RESOLUTION
Resolve to perform what you ought. Perform without fail what you resolve.

5. FRUGALITY
Make no expense but to do good to others or yourself: i.e., Waste nothing.

6. INDUSTRY
Lose no time. Be always employed in something useful. Cut off all unnecessary actions.

7. SINCERITY
Use no hurtful deceit. Think innocently and justly; and if you speak, speak accordingly.

8. JUSTICE
Wrong none, by doing injuries or omitting the benefits that are your duty.

9. MODERATION
Avoid extremes. Forbear resenting injuries so much as you think they deserve.

10. CLEANLINESS
Tolerate no uncleanness in body, clothes or habitation.

11. TRANQUILITY
Be not disturbed at trifles, or at accidents common or unavoidable.

12. CHASTITY
Rarely use venery but for health or offspring; never to dullness, weakness or the injury of your own or another's peace or reputation.

13. HUMILITY
Imitate Jesus and Socrates.

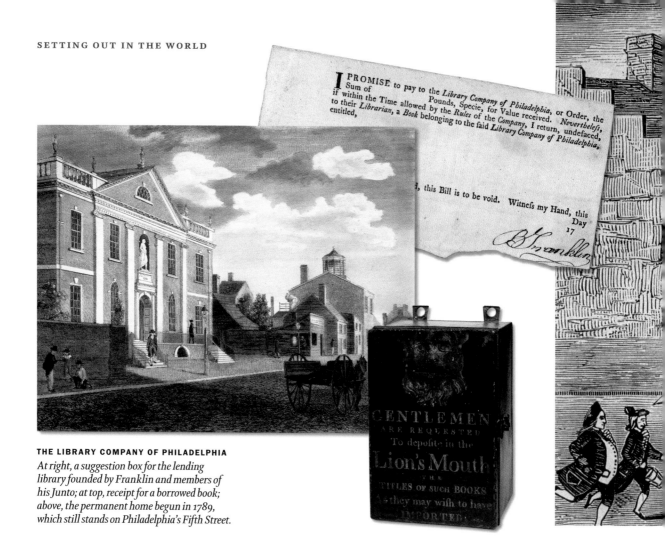

I PROMISE to pay to the *Library Company of Philadelphia*, or Order, the Sum of Pounds, Specie, for Value received. *Nevertheless,* if within the Time allowed by the Rules of the Company, I return, undefaced, to their *Librarian,* a *Book* belonging to the said *Library Company of Philadelphia,* entitled,

, this Bill is to be void. Witness my Hand, this Day 17

THE LIBRARY COMPANY OF PHILADELPHIA

At right, a suggestion box for the lending library founded by Franklin and members of his Junto; at top, receipt for a borrowed book; above, the permanent home begun in 1789, which still stands on Philadelphia's Fifth Street.

POOR RICHARD'S ALMANACK In 1732, not long after the birth of his second son, Franklin would embark on what would become one of the most important and lucrative projects of his life as a printer and public wit. Late in that year he began publishing *Poor Richard's Almanack*, an annual volume of weather forecasts, tide charts, homespun wisdom, and pithy proverbs that he would produce for 26 very profitable years.

Before he embarked on *Poor Richard's*, Franklin had for some time been the printer of almanacs produced by two other writers. But by the fall of 1732 he had lost both of those contracts. That was when he decided to put together his own, but with a distinct flavor. To that end, he created the fictional character Richard Saunders, borrowing the name from a celebrated English almanac writer. By calling him "Poor Richard" he also produced an echo of *Poor Robin's Almanack*, which was published in Newport, R.I., by his brother James. He equipped the comically put-upon Richard with a shrewish wife, Bridget, and a slyly self-deprecating wit.

Franklin had fun with Richard. To call attention to his new project, he launched an absurd feud with Titan Leeds, the publisher of a rival almanac. Writing under the cover of his Poor Richard pseudonym, he claimed in the preface to foresee the date of Leeds's death. The hapless Leeds took the bait. In the next edition of his own almanac, which appeared after the supposed date of his death, he published an angry reply, calling Franklin "a fool and a liar." A delighted Franklin/Richard replied in the following year's edition of his almanac that Leeds's intemperate statements proved he must have died as predicted. The real Leeds was too well-bred to use such language, Poor Richard declared, so some impostor must have written the attack.

Readers loved the almanacs not only for Richard's clever prefaces but also for the proverbs and maxims that were printed in the margins: "Early to bed and early to rise, makes a man healthy, wealthy and wise." "Fish and visitors stink in three days." "Three may keep a secret if two of them are dead." Many were old sayings that Franklin simply made sharper and funnier, but they helped to make his almanac a perennial bestseller. As the preface for its final edition, in 1758, Franklin produced a lengthy speech by a character he called "Father Abraham" who collected his aphorisms about thrift and hard work. It would later be published separately under the title *The Way to Wealth* and become the most frequently reprinted of all Franklin's works, including even the enormously popular *Autobiography*. And with that, the first business-advice bestseller was born.

THE VOLUNTEER MILITIA As he approached his forties Franklin enjoyed a succession of gratifying developments, including the birth in 1743 of a daughter, Sarah, called Sally, who would be his last child. In that year he also initiated another of his voluntary associations, one that would make a small contribution toward unifying the American colonies. The American Philosophical Society would allow thoughtful men from all up and down the Eastern seaboard to exchange ideas through the mail. The subjects could include natural science, manufacturing, maps and surveying, mathematics, animal husbandry, "and all philosophical experiments that let light into the nature of things."

2d PHILADELPHIA LOTTERY.
1748. CLASS the Third. No. 2103
This Billet entitles the Bearer to such Prize as may be drawn against its Number in the third Class (if demanded within Six Months after the last Drawing is finished) subject to no Deduction if under Twenty Pieces of Eight.

THE GREAT DEFENDER
The Grand Battery, at left, one of two forts built in 1747 as part of Franklin's plan to counter French and Spanish privateers who were raiding towns and ships along the Delaware River; above, a ticket for a lottery Franklin organized to raise money for the new colonial defenses

Franklin's most audacious proposal for a voluntary association would come four years later, and unlike the library or the fire brigade, this was an idea that posed at least a potential threat to the established authorities. By that time France and England had spent almost six decades embroiled in a succession of European wars that spilled over to the Americas. One of those, King George's War, was a four-year struggle that would begin in 1744 and even swept up Franklin's teenage son William, who marched off to join Pennsylvania forces fighting the French and Indians in Canada.

By 1747, French and Spanish privateers were attacking and robbing towns along the Delaware River. The Quaker leadership in the Pennsylvania Assembly, which had a traditional aversion to military force, dithered over raising funds to defend the exposed settlements. In the autumn of that year Franklin floated a new idea in his usual way, through a pamphlet, *Plain Truth*, written under the name "A Tradesman of Philadelphia." In it he argued that because both the Quakers and the wealthiest classes had failed to provide for the common defense, "the middling people, the farmers, shopkeepers and tradesmen," should step in. What he proposed was the formation of a volunteer militia, drawn from local citizenry, who would provide their own weapons and even elect their own officers.

When Franklin presented his idea at a public meeting in Philadelphia, it attracted more than 500 volunteers. Eventually there would be 10,000 from all around Pennsylvania. Though he declined the offer to appoint him colonel of the Philadelphia regiment, the militia made Franklin a hero throughout the colony. And this made him at the same time a threat to the Penns. In England, Thomas Penn responded to the news of Franklin's militia with trepidation. "This Association is founded on a contempt to government," he said, "and cannot end in anything but anarchy and confusion." As for Franklin, Penn had begun now to think of him as "a dangerous man."

So much the worse for Penn that Franklin's career as a public man was now getting seriously under way. In 1748, just 42 years old, Franklin retired from printing. He would leave day-to-day operation of his shop to his foreman, David Hall, while arranging to be paid half the firm's profits for 18 years. Though he would always hark back to an image of himself as a simple tradesman, Franklin would now become a gentleman, a man of leisure who could devote himself to scientific pursuits, to schemes for public improvement, and to the increasingly complex demands of the moment in which he lived. ■

EARLY RETIREMENT
As he neared retirement from his print shop at age 42, Franklin commissioned this portrait of himself in the costume of a gentleman.

Franklin's Idea of God

When Franklin was a boy, his father had hoped for a while that his precocious son might become a clergyman. While Franklin would grow up to be a kind of preacher, it would not be one in a clerical collar. But although he would never be conspicuously pious, and would certainly move far from the stern Calvinism of Cotton Mather, the preeminent religious figure in the Boston of his youth, he would grapple repeatedly with the question of God.

As a teenager Franklin was skeptical about the biblical God who reveals himself to mankind. He found himself attracted to the almost mechanistic God of deism, a sort of absentee landlord who creates the universe then steps aside, never intervening in human affairs. But faith in such an indifferent Supreme Being was not the kind that would offer people much incentive to be or to do good, which to the ever pragmatic Franklin were crucial benefits of religion. "I began to suspect that this doctrine, though it might be true, was not very useful."

By the age of 22 he had settled his thoughts sufficiently to produce what he called his "Articles of Belief and Acts of Religion." By that time he had decided there was "a Power above us" that delights in virtue but at the same time has little regard for humans and certainly no need to be worshiped by them. All the same, it was useful to *humans* to worship. It was, he concluded, "my duty as a man, to pay divine regards to *something*."

What form that worship took was of little concern to Franklin. Though he belonged to an Episcopalian congregation in Philadelphia, all his life he was opposed to religious sectarianism and intolerance of any kind. When his parents

MATHER *Franklin rejected his brand of faith.*

worried that he was straying too far from their own brand of religious orthodoxy, he wrote them a letter dismissing their concerns. "Scripture assures me that at the last day we shall not be examined by what we thought, but what we did."

In later life, and especially in connection with the events of the American Revolution, Franklin would speak more often of Providence, of God's guiding hand behind events. In 1789, when the deliberations of the Constitutional Convention began to seem hopelessly bogged down, he startled his fellow delegates by proposing that they begin their sessions with a prayer for divine guidance. In part because there was no money for a chaplain, the Convention rejected the idea.

R Franklin's Version of
The Lord's Prayer.

Heavenly Father, may all revere thee, and become thy dutiful Children & faithful Subjects; may thy Laws be obeyed on Earth perfectly as they are in Heaven: Provide for us this Day as thou hast hitherto daily done: Forgive us our Trespasses, and enable us likewise to forgive those that offend us. Keep us out of Temptation, & deliver us from Evil.

Always ready to improve the world around him, in the 1740s Franklin revised the best-known Christian prayer to make it more clear and accurate. So "lead us not into temptation" becomes "keep us out of temptation" because he believed temptation came from Satan, not God.

OLD VERSION:
1. *Our Father which art in Heaven.*
2. *Hallowed be thy Name.*
3. *Thy Kingdom come.*
4. *Thy Will be done on Earth as it is in Heaven.*
5. *Give us this Day our daily Bread.*
6. *Forgive us our Debts as we forgive our Debtors.*
7. *And lead us not into Temptation, but deliver us from Evil.*

FRANKLIN'S VERSION:
1. *Heavenly Father,*
2. *May all revere thee,*
3. *And become thy dutiful Children and faithful Subjects.*
4. *May thy Laws be obeyed on Earth as perfectly as they are in Heaven.*
5. *Provide for us this Day as thou has hither to daily done.*
6. *Forgive us our Trespasses, and enable us likewise to forgive those that offend us.*
7. *Keep us out of Temptation, and deliver us from Evil.*

Just one month before he died, Franklin made a final summation of his beliefs in a letter to the Rev. Ezra Stiles, president of Yale, who had written him to ask if he would set out his thoughts on religion. Franklin opened his reply with a credo not so different from the one he had arrived at in his twenties. "I believe in one God, creator of the Universe. That he governs it by his Providence. That he ought to be worshipped. That the most acceptable service we render to him is doing good to his other children. That the soul of man is immortal and will be treated with justice in another life respecting its conduct in this."

But Stiles had also asked Franklin to specify his views on Christ. To that question Franklin replied with care. "I think the system of morals and his religion, as he left them to us, the best the world ever saw or is likely to see." But after also observing that the Christian faith had suffered "various corrupting changes," he admitted to "some doubts as to his divinity." Then he added, with the wry equanimity of a man at the very end of his life, that he had never really studied the question, "and think it needless to busy myself with it now, when I expect soon an opportunity of knowing the truth with less trouble." ∎

MOVING INTO
A WIDER SPHERE

Retirement for Franklin did not mean a retreat from the world. Far from it. The most eventful period of his life was still ahead of him, years in which he would make some of his most important scientific discoveries and shape events as never before.

One of his earliest accomplishments was to establish in Philadelphia the city's first academy of higher learning. Franklin had been thinking for years about how to improve the schooling available in his adopted town. As an initial step, in 1749 he published a pamphlet that got wide circulation in Pennsylvania. It outlined in great detail his ideas on why such a school was needed and how it should be organized and funded. And what should it teach? "Those things that are likely to be most useful," he explained, including arithmetic, grammar, classics, history, geography, and public speaking—a skill that Franklin, this most public of men, would never truly master. The young men at his proposed school would be "frequently exercis'd in running, leaping, wrestling" and, of course, Franklin's favorite pastime—"swimming." And unlike the other major colonial colleges, Harvard, Yale, Princeton, and William & Mary, the school would be nonsectarian, the first such college in America.

Franklin's proposals found enough support among prosperous Philadelphians that money was quickly raised to establish the school. The donors then elected a board of trustees and, naturally,

THE HOUSE THAT BEN BUILT
Pennsylvania Hospital, a Franklin project, as it appeared in 1755, two years after it admitted its first patients

sylvania   *Hospital, with the Elevation of the*

any private   *Persons, Was Piously founded, for the Relief of the*

Built A Dom.   *1755.*   *from Nº 1 to 2*

TAKE CARE OF HIM
& I WILL REPAY
THEE

made Franklin president. In turn he negotiated to acquire a home for the school—the Great Hall that had been built for the Rev. George Whitefield, an English evangelist who had electrified the colonies a decade earlier during the religious revival known as the Great Awakening. After some renovations the new academy opened its doors early in 1751. A college aimed at older students was chartered five years later. In 1791 that college would assume the name it still bears—the University of Pennsylvania.

Very soon Franklin was on to his next civic improvement, a public hospital for the poor. As he explains in the *Autobiography*, the idea was proposed to him by a friend, Dr. Thomas Bond, who had studied medicine in London and Paris and learned there about the emerging idea of modern hospitals. On his return to Philadelphia, Bond was troubled by the number of unhealthy poor folk, some of them mentally disturbed, wandering the city streets. But he was unable to raise funds for his own hospital until Franklin promoted the idea in newspaper pieces and drummed up a subscriber fund. When the money stream began to slow, the ever resourceful Franklin conceived a new idea—having the Pennsylvania Assembly promise to provide £2,000 if the same amount could first be raised in private

donations. With that he invented the matching grant. As he put it, this would provide donors with "an additional motive to give, since every man's donation would be doubled." The matching scheme was a success, and the hospital—America's first—began admitting patients in 1753. It survives to this day as Pennsylvania Hospital.

THE PENNSYLVANIA ASSEMBLYMAN A pivotal transition in Franklin's life began in 1751, when he assumed a seat in the Pennsylvania Assembly after the death of one of its members. Franklin had been clerk of the Assembly, an unelected post, since 1736. As clerk he could not take part in debates, and he found the job tedious enough at times that he spent hours devising mathematical puzzles on paper. But as he explained in his *Autobiography*, the clerkship was useful in helping him to secure "the business of printing the votes, laws, paper money and other occasional jobs for the public that, on the whole, were very profitable."

But to become a sitting member of the Assembly, one of just 26, meant that now Franklin would not merely observe debates but very often dominate them. And while he had long been a civic leader in Philadelphia, now he would be prominently involved in the affairs of Pennsylvania and, in time, the other colonies. As he put it: "I conceived my becoming a member would enlarge my power of doing good. I would not however insinuate that my ambition was not flattered by all these promotions. It certainly was. For considering my low beginning they were great things to me." He also took the opportunity to install his son William as the new clerk.

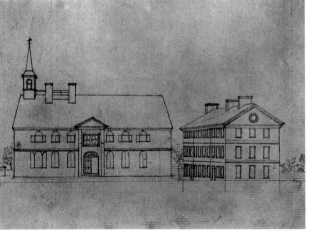

FROM SERMONS TO LESSONS
The first home of Franklin's academy, above at left, was a hall originally built for the charismatic evangelist George Whitefield, at top.

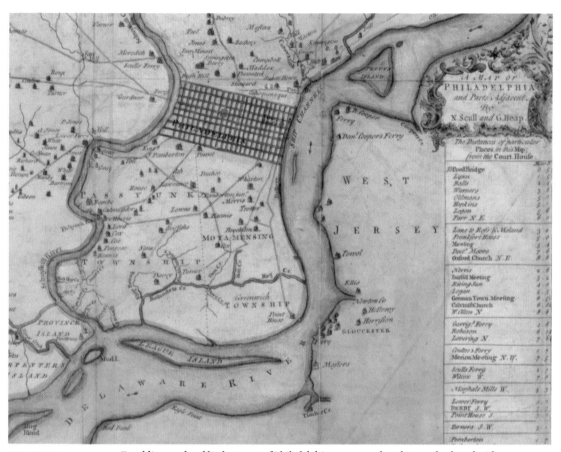

LET THERE BE LIGHTING *Franklin paved and lit the streets of Philadelphia, represented on this map by the red grid.*

Pennsylvania politics were some of the most turbulent of any of the American colonies. By the mid-18th century, Pennsylvania was one of just three colonies—Delaware and Maryland were the others—that remained a land grant from the crown of England to a single family, who ruled through an appointed governor. In 1681, Charles II had given the territory to William Penn in payment for a debt owed to Penn's father. Though Penn would establish a colony there as a refuge for his fellow Quakers, most of his descendants would return to the Church of England. To them the colony was not so much a "holy experiment" as a source of revenue, most of it coming from the sale of land to new settlers. This led to continual tension between the "Proprietors," as the London-based Penns were called, and Pennsylvania's Quaker-dominated Assembly, especially over the Penns' resistance to paying taxes on their vast landholdings. For the next two decades many of Franklin's opinions and actions would be driven by hostility to the Proprietors and a desire to transfer Pennsylvania to the direct control of the British crown.

But first Franklin would busy himself in the Assembly with more mundane matters, like cleaning and lighting the streets of Philadelphia. He was appointed to a committee that produced a report in favor of issuing paper currency, an idea he had long promoted as a way to put more money into circulation. And he continued to work as a journalist, pamphleteer, and polemicist. In one satirical piece he published under a pseudonym in the *Gazette* he attacked the British policy of exiling criminals to America, which the colonists blamed for their high crime rates, by proposing that the colonies should export rattlesnakes to England. At least, he observed, "the rattlesnake gives warning before he attempts his mischief, which the convict does not."

When Sparks Flew

By Frederic Golden

It's an iconic moment in American history studied by generations of schoolkids. On a storm-tossed June day in 1752, Ben Franklin, joined by his son William, hoisted a kite with a wire poking out of it high over Philadelphia. As the skies darkened, the kite's hemp string bristled with electricity, like a cat's fur after being stroked. Franklin brought his knuckles close to a brass key dangling from the end of the string. A spark leaped through the air, giving him a powerful jolt—and immeasurable pleasure. No longer could anyone doubt that the small electrical charges created in popular 18th-century parlor games and the Jovian bolts thundering from the heavens were one and the same.

But is this oft-told tale another Founders myth, like Washington's confessing to axing his father's cherry tree? In 2003 a book titled *Bolt of Fate* attempted to prove the whole thing was a hoax, somewhat like the spoofs Franklin confected for *Poor Richard's Almanack*. Author Tom Tucker's evidence, however, was slim. He made much of the improbability of flying a kite weighted down by a heavy key, ignoring Franklin's long history of kite flying, and of his delay in publicizing the experiment, though only three months elapsed. More to the point, scientific fraud seems wildly out of character for Franklin. As Harvard chemist and Franklin buff Dudley Herschbach, a Nobel laureate, notes, "It would have been utterly inconsistent with all of his other work in [science] for him to claim he'd done something he had not."

The larger issue, however, is not whether Ben flew the kite, which most scholars agree he did, but how significant his experiment was. In fact, many of his scientific breakthroughs were of great import—and he had a selfless urge to share his new knowledge. When Franklin caught the electricity bug in his forties, "electrick fire" was a playful if puzzling entertainment. His experiments led him to startlingly modern conclusions. The "fire," he said, is a single "fluid," not the dual "vitreous" and "resinous" electricities postulated by European savants. It exists in two states: plus and minus (terms he coined, along with positive and negative, battery and conductor). Further, he said, if there is an excess of charge in one conductor, it must be precisely balanced by a deficit in another. Stated another way, electrical charge is always conserved, an important new principle descended from Newton's conservation of momentum. Finally, he said, when sparks fly between two charged bodies, they instantly restore the equilibrium between them.

Franklin wasn't the first to propose a kinship between harmless sparks and a lightning bolt. But he was the first to suggest an experiment to prove it. The Royal Society of London published his proposal, yet it was the French who actually put it to the test. The experiment Franklin proposed, which he first revealed in a letter to his English agent in July 1750, called for installing on a high place, like a steeple, a sentry box with a metal pole extending from its roof. If an electrified storm cloud passed overhead, Franklin said, the pole—preferably sharpened at the end—would pull out a small amount of the cloud's "fire." Or to put it in modern terms, it would induce an electrical charge in the pole. An observer in the sentry box could detect the charge by touching the pole with an insulated ground wire and drawing sparks. Or if the pole itself was grounded, it would extract all the cloud's "fire" in a lightning bolt and sweep it harmlessly into the earth. Franklin had created the lightning rod.

"...as we enjoy great advantages from the inventions of others, we should be glad of an opportunity to serve others by any invention of ours ..."

— BENJAMIN FRANKLIN, *from his* Autobiography

But before Franklin learned, late in August 1752, of the French success with his experiment that spring (and of the king's compliments to Monsieur Franklin), he set about undertaking it himself in June of that year—with a special wrinkle. The steeple he had hoped to use was unfinished, and he decided he could prove his case just as easily with a wired kite. It would rise even higher in the sky. So why did he do it on the sly? Joseph Priestley, the British chemist and a Franklin crony, later explained, "... dreading the ridicule which too commonly attends unsuccessful attempts in science, he communicated his intended experiment to nobody but his son, who assisted him in raising the kite."

When the secret finally got out, it had sweeping repercussions. Franklin's experiment showed that electricity was not just an amusement but a force of nature, like gravity. It also illustrated an Enlightenment ideal: that pure science—science done for the joy of exploring nature—could have enormous practical consequences, as shown by the lightning rod. The invention drastically reduced the threat of fire to churches and other tall structures. Most profoundly, it shook the belief that lightning was a sign of God's displeasure.

What Franklin modestly described as his "electrical amusements" made him the world's most famous scientist. The German philosopher Immanuel Kant called him the "new Prometheus." Most important, Franklin's fame helped open French hearts—and purse strings— when years later he came calling at Louis XVI's court on behalf of his embattled young nation. As the French financier Turgot would say of the kite flier from Philadelphia, "He snatched lightning from the sky and the scepter from tyrants." ∎

THE SCIENTIST

It was Franklin's scientific discoveries, especially in the field of electricity, that first made him famous on both sides of the Atlantic. As his acute biographer Gordon S. Wood writes in *The Americanization of Benjamin Franklin*: "Franklin began to emerge as a symbol of the primitive New World's capacity to produce an untutored genius." But electricity, a subject that fascinated the 18th century, was just one of his many interests. And being the practical man he was, whenever possible he turned his research into inventions for the improvement of everyday life.

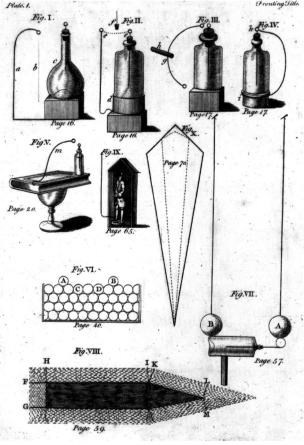

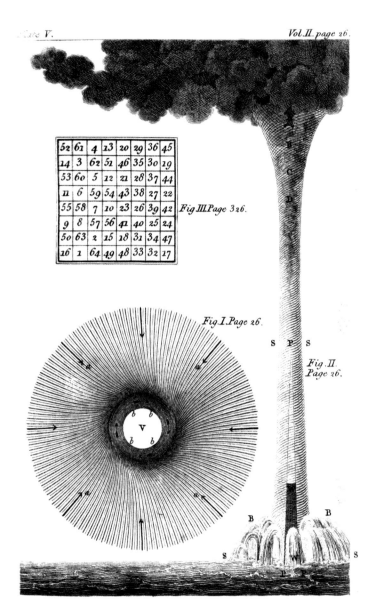

Plate V.　Vol. II. page 26.

52	61	4	13	20	29	36	45
14	3	62	51	46	35	30	19
53	60	5	12	21	28	37	44
11	6	59	54	43	38	27	22
55	58	7	10	23	26	39	42
9	8	57	56	41	40	25	24
50	63	2	15	18	31	34	47
16	1	64	49	48	33	32	17

Fig III Page 326.

Fig.I.Page 26.

Fig.II.
Page 26.

ELECTRICITY

(clockwise from top left)

SUPERMODELS: *Franklin used these to demonstrate the effectiveness of his lightning rod.*

CRUCIAL POINT: *"A rod of iron," Franklin wrote, "sharpened gradually to a point like a needle," could draw lightning away from a building into the ground.*

TOWERS OF POWER: *As a step toward inventing the battery, he joined "Leyden jars" that collect electrical charges.*

MECHANICS ILLUSTRATED: *Drawings from his book* Experiments and Observations on Electricity

CHARGE IT: *Franklin devised a hand-cranked wooden machine like this one to produce and collect static charges.*

WATERSPOUTS

On his transatlantic voyages Franklin had the opportunity to observe waterspouts— rotating vortexes of water vapor that descend from clouds. He produced this diagram to accompany his speculations on what causes them. Beside the spout appears one of his mathematical puzzles called a magic square.

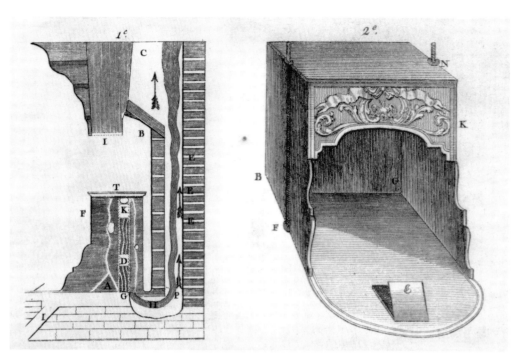

THE STOVE

Fireplaces are an inefficient way to heat a room. In 1742, Franklin invented a stove intended to force more heat forward while carrying smoke away. Though his original design couldn't generate enough airflow, it was a step in the development of more efficient home heating. Offered a lucrative patent, Franklin instead placed his invention in the public domain.

MUSIC OF THE (HEMI) SPHERES

Franklin was inspired to devise his ingenious "armonica" by the common practice of rubbing the rim of a wine glass to produce a musical tone. The player used a crank to turn the glass bowls, which were "played" with a wet finger. Both Mozart and Beethoven composed works for it.

CHARTING THE STREAM
Franklin was fascinated by the Gulf Stream, the powerful Atlantic current that flows east. He asked his cousin, a sea captain, to map its course, then published the map in 1786.

DOUBLE DUTY
By fitting it with a set of short steps on a hinge, Franklin adapted a conventional chair so that it could also serve as a library ladder.

Pl. I. *A Magic Square of Squares.*

200	217	232	249	8	25	40	57	72	89	104	121	136	153	168	185
58	39	26	7	250	231	218	199	186	167	154	135	122	103	90	71
198	219	230	251	6	27	38	59	70	91	102	123	134	155	166	187
60	37	28	5	252	229	220	197	188	165	156	133	124	101	92	69
201	216	233	248	9	24	41	56	73	88	105	120	137	152	169	184
55	42	23	10	247	234	215	202	183	170	151	138	119	106	87	74
203	214	235	246	11	22	43	54	75	86	107	118	139	150	171	182
53	44	21	12	245	236	213	204	181	172	149	140	117	108	85	76
205	212	237	244	13	20	45	52	77	84	109	116	141	148	173	180
51	46	19	14	243	238	211	206	179	174	147	142	115	110	83	78
207	210	239	242	15	18	47	50	79	82	111	114	143	146	175	178
49	48	17	16	241	240	209	208	177	176	145	144	113	112	81	80
196	221	228	253	4	29	36	61	68	93	100	125	132	157	164	189
62	35	30	3	254	227	222	195	190	163	158	131	126	99	94	67
194	223	226	255	2	31	34	63	66	95	98	127	130	159	162	191
64	33	32	1	256	225	224	193	192	161	160	129	128	97	96	65

B. Franklin invt. I. Ferguson delin.   *J. Mynde sc.*

The great Square is divided into 256 small squares; in which, all the numbers from 1 to 256 are so placed as to have the following Properties.

1. The sum of all the 16 Numbers, in any column, horizontal or vertical, is 2056.
2. The sum of half a column, either horizontal or Vertical, is 1028, the half of 2056.
3. The sum in any oblique line ascending, added to that in the oblique line descending from it, is 2056.
4. The sum of all the numbers added together in the 4 little squares next the 4 corners, is 2056.
5. If a square hole (as below) be cut in a piece of paper, of such a size as to take in just 16 of the small squares, and be laid upon any part of the great Square; the sum of all the 16 numbers seen through the hole will be 2056, the same as in any column.

	244	13	20	45	
The Hole	14	243	238	211	2056
	242	15	10	47	
	16	241	240	209	

TAKE A NUMBER
Franklin loved to come up with "magic squares" like this one, which he designed around 1760. The sum of all 16 numbers in any row or diagonal amounts to 2,056. So does the sum of any square of 16 cells.

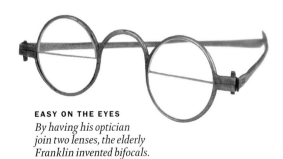

EASY ON THE EYES
By having his optician join two lenses, the elderly Franklin invented bifocals.

CELEBRITY SCIENTIST *In this portrait of Franklin the lightning rod that secured his international fame is seen behind him.*

It was also in 1751 that Franklin produced a notable pamphlet, *Observations Concerning the Increase of Mankind, Peopling of Countries, Etc.*, in which he argued that the abundance of inexpensive land for farming helped to explain why Americans married earlier and had more children than Europeans. He predicted that the population of the colonies would double every 20 years until they became larger than Britain in 100 years—a forecast that proved remarkably accurate. But Franklin, still a loyal subject of the king, did not envision this abundant future nation as a competitor with Britain. Rather he imagined it as a coequal located firmly within the grand enterprise of the British Empire. It would be decades before Franklin could imagine an America detached from its motherland across the Atlantic.

RISING TROUBLES ON THE FRONTIER In the 1750s the most pressing of Pennsylvania's affairs was security in its Western regions, a question Franklin had first addressed with his formation of the volunteer militias in the previous decade. French traders and soldiers were penetrating the Ohio Valley as part of a plan to build a line of forts from Canada to Louisiana, thereby confining the British colonies to the Eastern Seaboard. Despite escalating hostilities with the French and their Indian allies, the Quaker majority in the Pennsylvania Assembly, pacifist on principle and stingy by instinct, was reluctant to spend on frontier defenses.

In their competition with the French the Pennsylvanians had Indian allies of their own, notably the Six Nations of the Iroquois Confederacy. They also had the grudging support of the Delaware Indians—grudging because the Delaware carried bitter memories of "The Walking Purchase" of 1737. In that year Thomas Penn invoked (or fabricated) an old agreement with the tribe that gave his father title to tribal land amounting to the distance a man could cover on foot in a day and a half. Instead of walking for the appointed time Penn hired three runners, allowing him to claim far more land than the Indians had expected.

Hoping to stabilize its tribal alliances, in the autumn of 1753 Pennsylvania sent a delegation of three commissioners, including Franklin, to meet with the leaders of the Delaware and other tribes. The conference was held at Carlisle, a site midway between Philadelphia and the Ohio River. It produced limited results. The Indians wanted all white settlers to retreat east of the Appalachians. They also wanted colonial traders to supply them with more guns and less rum—alcohol was something they couldn't resist but couldn't handle. The Pennsylvania delegation did little more than promise to restrain their traders. When they got home they also wrote a report on the proceedings lambasting the increasing sale of liquor to the natives, so as "to keep these poor Indians continually under the force of liquor."

On his return from Carlisle, Franklin learned that he had been appointed by the British to share a job he had long been seeking—deputy postmaster for the colonies. In that position he would introduce improvements that made postal service faster and more reliable, drawing the colonies closer together. He would also eventually earn an additional handsome living for himself and place friends and relatives in jobs all around the colonies. (For one thing, he made his son William postmaster of Philadelphia.) No less important, his inspection tours of postal routes all up and down the Eastern Seaboard gave him a more comprehensive sense of the colonies and strengthened his notion of their common destiny.

TOWARD A MORE UNIFIED AMERICA At around the same time that the Carlisle conference was concluding, the governor of Virginia sent a 21-year-old major in the Virginia militia named George Washington into the Ohio Valley to demand the departure of French forces there. Washington's mission ended in a rout, but he would return the next spring to mount a series of raids against the French. These would eventually escalate into the French and Indian War.

In response to the growing hostilities, early in 1754 the British authorities called for a meeting in Albany, N.Y., of representatives from all the colonies to discuss possibilities for cooperation among them. In the end only seven took part, but one of them was Pennsylvania, which sent a four-member delegation. Naturally it included Franklin, who was determined to do what he could to promote an idea much more thoroughgoing than mere cooperation—colonial union.

As early as 1751, in a letter to a friend, Franklin had sketched out a structure for a unified colonial body that would deal with common defense and relations with the Indians. He proposed a council of delegates chosen by the colonial assemblies in numbers roughly proportionate to the share of taxes

MAKING THE ROUNDS *A 20th-century artist imagines the well-traveled Franklin on one of his postal inspection tours.*

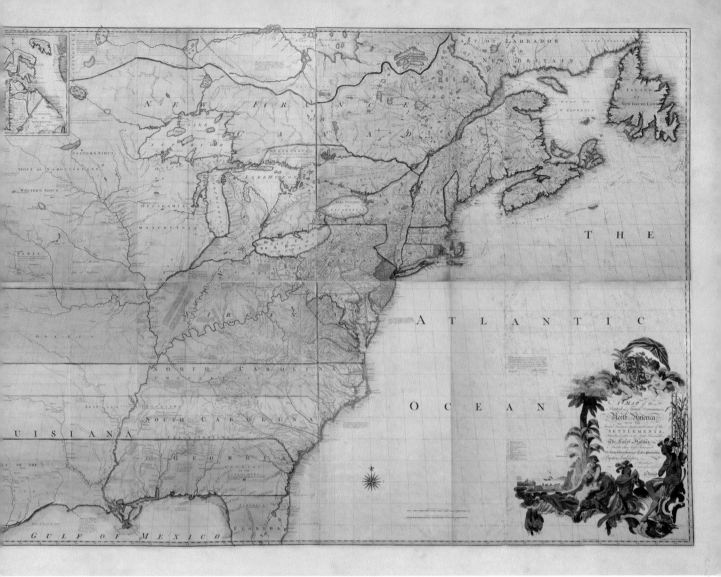

each colony would pay to a common treasury. The council would be headed by a governor appointed by the king and would rotate its regular meetings among cities throughout the colonies. At the time he also envisioned that the council would be formed by the colonies themselves, not imposed by the British.

Working in tandem with Thomas Hutchinson, a delegate from Massachusetts, Franklin submitted a proposal to the Albany Congress similar in many respects to the one outlined in his letter. But now, because he doubted the colonies had the will to unify themselves, he proposed that the plan could be imposed by the crown. It was a vain hope. Though the Congress adopted his plan, not one of the colonial assemblies did. The British, who had their own reasons to resist the idea of a unified America, rejected it as well.

The following summer Britain decided to act unilaterally. It sent Gen. Edward Braddock to expel the French. With two regiments of redcoats under his command, the 60-year-old Braddock had nothing but contempt for the French and their Indian allies. "These savages," he told Franklin, "may indeed be a formidable enemy to your raw American militia. But upon the King's regular and disciplined troops, sir, it is impossible they would make any impression."

THE BIG COUNTRY
Franklin was very familiar with this map produced by the Virginia-born physician and cartographer Dr. John Mitchell in 1755. Mitchell drew it to alert the British to French encroachments on the extensive interior lands claimed by Britain's colonies. After the Revolutionary War, updated versions of the same map were consulted repeatedly in the peace talks that Franklin and others conducted with British negotiators.

59

THE DEFENDER *A mural shows Franklin directing fort construction.*

"It is supposed an undoubted right of Englishmen not to be taxed but by their own consent given through their representatives."

—BENJAMIN FRANKLIN, *in a 1754 letter to Massachusetts Gov. William Shirley that foreshadowed a major issue of the American Revolution*

It was a foolish boast. In July Braddock and his men would be cut to pieces by a force of French and Indians near Fort Duquesne. A badly wounded Braddock would die a few days later. When the French and Indians followed up with a campaign of terror against the Western settlers, an army of refugees descended upon Philadelphia. In *The First American: The Life and Times of Benjamin Franklin*, the historian H.W. Brands quotes a letter written by Richard Peters, Pennsylvania's provincial secretary, describing the dire situation. "The roads are full of starved, naked, indigent multitudes."

By now the Quaker majority in the Pennsylvania Assembly had grasped the need to fund colonial defenses. But their plan for doing that produced a bill that would tax the lands held by the Proprietors, and as always the Penns wouldn't hear of it. When the provincial governor, Robert Morris, vetoed the bill, Franklin was chosen to take the Assembly's part in an increasingly heated correspondence with Morris in which Franklin gave full vent to his exasperation with the Proprietors.

Meanwhile, the colony still needed to be defended. So Franklin worked up a plan for another militia, this one sanctioned, as his first had not been, by the provincial government. Franklin himself led 50 militiamen on horseback to Pennsylvania's northwest frontier to organize defenses and construct several forts. Later he was elected colonel of the Philadelphia regiment, which escorted him with drawn swords through the streets of the city. This was an episode that greatly displeased Thomas Penn when word of it reached him in London. Drawn swords—was this puffed-up tradesman beginning to fancy himself a colonial potentate? Even friends worried that Franklin was overdoing it. But Franklin was unfazed. "The people happen to love me," he wrote to one of them. "Perhaps that's my fault."

The people might have loved Franklin. Penn, certainly, did not. So much the worse then that he would soon be dealing with the man in person. In 1757 the Assembly decided to dispatch an emissary to London to argue its case on taxes directly to the Proprietors, and if that brought no satisfaction, to appeal to the British government. Who better to send than the Penns' most forceful antagonist? That summer Franklin would board ship for London. Accompanying him would be his son William, then about 27. Claiming that she feared ocean crossings, his wife, Deborah, would stay home. Franklin appears to have made no great effort to change her mind. ∎

CRISIS AND RESPONSE
In 1755, British forces advancing into the Ohio River Valley were ambushed and overwhelmed by the French and their Indian allies. Gen. Edward Braddock, seen seated at top, was mortally wounded. Below, Franklin returns to Philadelphia escorted by his militia regiment.

OUR MAN IN LONDON

Franklin and William arrived in London in July 1757. They quickly found lodgings with Margaret Stevenson, called Peggy, a widow living with her 18-year-old daughter Mary, known as Polly, in a four-story row house at 7 Craven Street. Franklin would remain with the Stevensons for the entire 16 years of his two successive stays in London. Mother and daughter would become for him a surrogate family. He may well have conducted an affair with Peggy—we have no clear evidence—but he plainly developed something of an infatuation with Polly.

The Penns took a caustic view of the man coming from Philadelphia to confront them. "Franklin's popularity is nothing here," Thomas Penn assured Pennsylvania's provincial secretary, Richard Peters. "He will be looked upon coldly by great people." Franklin quickly got his first taste of just how coldly. Before he could meet with Penn, he was summoned before Lord Granville, head of the Privy Council, which was made up of the closest advisers of King George II. Granville—who also happened to be the brother-in-law of Thomas Penn—abruptly informed Franklin, "You Americans have wrong ideas of the nature of your constitution." The instructions given to colonial governors were law, Granville told him, and colonial assemblies could not defy them. When Franklin protested that the colonial charters provided for laws to be made by their own legislatures, Granville insisted Franklin was wrong.

Soon after, Franklin began meeting with Thomas Penn and his brother Richard. At their request he drew up for them a list of complaints by the Pennsylvania Assembly. The Penns turned the list over to Britain's attorney general and its solicitor general for their opinions. Meanwhile, the Penns played a waiting game, stalling in the hope that Franklin would simply go home.

Matters came to a head during a bitter meeting between Franklin and Thomas Penn in January 1758. In that heated conversation, which Franklin

THE MAN OF AFFAIRS
Franklin was so pleased by David Martin's 1767 portrait, which depicts him as a thinker and writer, that he had a copy made and sent it to his wife in Philadelphia.

later set down in writing, he insisted that Penn's father, William, had granted the Pennsylvania Assembly the powers of a parliament. Thomas replied that the royal charter by which his father had established the colony did not permit him to convey that authority. Franklin pointed out that in that case William had deceived the settlers who came to Pennsylvania believing he had. Thomas shrugged. "The royal charter was no secret," he said. "If they were deceived it was their own fault."

Franklin was furious and vented his anger later in a letter in which he described their confrontation as a moment when he conceived "a more cordial and thorough contempt for [Penn] than I have ever before felt for any man living." It wasn't long before Penn learned of the letter, which confirmed him in a decision to refuse all further dealings with the haughty Pennsylvanian. As for Franklin, figuring there was little to keep him in London for now, he headed off to spend the summer of 1758 on a more agreeable mission—traveling around England with his son William to be hosted by his many admirers.

FIGHTING THE PENNS That summer father and son visited Ecton, the Franklin family's ancestral village, and spent time at Cambridge University, where Franklin collaborated with the scientist John Hadley on experiments concerning evaporation. But if it was a sweet summer, the autumn would be less so. In November the Penns finally made their reply to the Assembly's complaints in letters that reaffirmed their insistence that any instructions they gave to their governors could not be ignored by the Assembly. They did allow that some of their properties might be taxable, but they made no promises. And one other thing. They specified that they would not deal anymore with Franklin. The Assembly would need to choose another representative.

When this news reached Franklin, he made a radical proposal to the Assembly. Why not seek to have Parliament transfer Pennsylvania out of the Proprietors' control and make it a British royal colony? Franklin was still devoted to Britain and its empire, in which he imagined a fast-growing America as an important partner. It was a loyalty that blinded him to the fact that the king's ministers were no more willing than the Penns to confer sovereign authority upon colonial legislatures.

Having persuaded the Assembly to go along with his plan, Franklin spent much of the year that followed trying to press various cases against the Proprietors in the Privy Council, mostly in vain. He consoled himself in the summer of 1759 with another round of travels with William, this time to

THE "PROPRIETOR" *Thomas Penn would be Franklin's first great antagonist in London.*

"I have long [believed] that the foundations of the future grandeur and stability of the British Empire lie in America."

—BENJAMIN FRANKLIN, *writing in 1760*

Scotland, where he was received as an intellectual luminary and became friends with such notables as the economist Adam Smith and the philosopher David Hume. On the same gratifying trip, the University of St. Andrews awarded him the honorary doctorate that gave him the right to be called Dr. Franklin, a title he was generally known by from then on.

Early the next year William proved to be very much his father's son—just like Franklin, he fathered a son out of wedlock, by a woman who may have been a prostitute. While William acknowledged that the boy was his, he wanted the matter kept secret. So for the first years of his life, William Temple Franklin, called Temple, would be raised away from London by a series of foster caretakers.

Despite his lack of success in turning the Privy Council against the Penns, Franklin had not given up hope that the Britain he so admired would be the answer to Pennsylvania's problems with the Proprietors. When George III was crowned in September 1761, Franklin and his son rushed back from a trip to Holland and Flanders to attend the coronation. Ever the loyal Briton, Franklin allowed himself to hope that George III—the very man who would later prosecute Britain's war against the rebellious colonies—would be sympathetic to his case for making Pennsylvania a crown colony.

But the new king *would* look favorably on Franklin's son. In the summer of 1762, William, who was about 30 years old, was appointed royal governor of New Jersey. No doubt this was done in part to secure the loyalty of his influential father. As for William, his affection for England was wholehearted. During his years in London, while he studied law, he had become increasingly charmed by the wealthy and well-born social circles that gave him entry, if only because he was the son of such a famous father.

Franklin's London

By the time Franklin made his second trip to London, in 1757, it was a great metropolis with 750,000 people, the second-largest city in the world after Beijing. A vital, cosmopolitan place, growing explosively, it drew people from all around Britain's vast empire. Great squares and crescents were being constructed in elegant new neighborhoods like the West End. New roadways across the Thames, like the Westminster Bridge, were opening up South London for development.

For a man with Franklin's capacious mind, the intellectual life of London was an immense treat. Much of it centered around coffeehouses, where people gathered to sip coffee, read newspapers, and discuss the events of the day. This was the London of Samuel Johnson and his biographer James Boswell, of the poet and playwright Oliver Goldsmith, of the statesman and philosopher Edmund Burke. Franklin would become friends with Burke and acquainted with Boswell, who would describe the sociable American in his journal as "all jollity and pleasantry." But London was also a place where great wealth co-existed with the most degrading poverty and all the problems of rapid growth. The smoke from heating fires that hung constantly over the city was infamous. Franklin complained of it in a letter to his wife, Deborah. "The whole town is one great smoky house, and every street a chimney, the air full of floating sea-coal soot, and you never get a sweet breath of what is pure, without riding some miles for it into the country."

MR. FRANKLIN'S NEIGHBORHOOD
The house where Franklin rented rooms was near the Strand, seen here, which in the 18th century was emerging as one of the city's great commercial streets, though also still a haunt of prostitutes and pickpockets. This painting by Canaletto shows Northumberland House, home to one of England's richest families until it was torn down in 1874. At top left, Franklin's calling card.

THE SON ALSO RISES
*Franklin's son William would be named
royal governor of New Jersey.*

Very soon William was drawn even more tightly to Britain when he became engaged to a young Englishwoman, Elizabeth Downes, the daughter of a Barbados plantation owner. Though Franklin claimed to approve the union, he didn't bother to attend the September wedding. Two weeks earlier he had boarded yet another ship, this one taking him back to Philadelphia. A few months later William and his new bride would follow, leaving Temple behind, for now, in England.

TROUBLED DAYS AT HOME Franklin arrived back in Philadelphia in November 1762. But after the excitements of London he was soon restless there. "To me the streets seem thinner of people," he wrote to a British friend, Richard Jackson, "owing perhaps to my being so long accustomed to the bustling crowded streets of London." In April he set off on a lengthy inspection tour of postal routes throughout the colonies, some of it in the company of his daughter Sally. Over seven months he would cover a 1,780-mile circuit from Virginia to New Hampshire.

In what may have been a sign that he had given up hope that Deborah could ever be persuaded to return with him to London, Franklin also began planning a new house on Market Street. Did he imagine himself spending much time there? His letters to friends in England are full of longing for London. What we know is that his return to North America would be brief, just two years.

Brief, but eventful. By the end of 1763, Pennsylvania was in the grip of another political crisis emanating out of its Western territories. Even after the end of the French and Indian War, members of the Ottawa tribe continued to conduct raids on Western forts and settlements. In a brutal reprisal, in

In a 1764 cartoon, Franklin, in the foreground, hopes to benefit from the Paxton Boys crisis while Quakers worry. In a pamphlet, right, Franklin's enemies publicize his son's illegitimate birth.

December a band of 57 white settlers from around the town of Paxton massacred six peaceful Indians. Another 14 died in a second massacre two weeks later. A burgeoning frontier mob were soon calling themselves the Paxton Boys and threatening to carry their vigilante campaign into Philadelphia, where 140 Indians were being sheltered. The frontiersmen swore to kill not only them but also any whites who tried to protect them. Franklin had no hesitations about recommending harsh policies toward Indian tribes on the warpath. But the slaughter of peaceful Indians appalled him. In response he wrote and circulated an impassioned pamphlet that described the killings in detail. "Men, women and little children—were every one inhumanly murdered—in cold blood!"

The pamphlet helped to spur formation of a militia to stop the Paxton Boys before they could reach Philadelphia. But before resorting to confrontation, Pennsylvania governor John Penn decided to send a delegation that included Franklin to talk with the frontiersmen, who were camped just north of the city. Remarkably, at the meeting the insurgents were persuaded to go home. Franklin later described the whirlwind episode in a letter to a friend in London. "Your old friend was a common soldier, a counselor, a kind of dictator, an ambassador to the country mob, and on their returning home, nobody, again."

69

ALL BROKEN UP *A cartoon by Franklin shows how the Stamp Act would sever the colonies from Britain and damage both.*

Franklin's entente with the governor was short-lived. In March 1764 he pushed through 26 resolutions in the Assembly denouncing government by the Proprietors. Next he circulated a petition calling for the transfer of the colony to royal rule, organized meetings and rallies in support of the idea, and published dozens of articles and pamphlets to promote it. But Franklin was misreading public opinion. Direct British rule was not an option with wide appeal among Pennsylvanians. For one thing, in a colony that prided itself on its religious freedoms, many feared it could mean imposition of the Church of England as the established faith. And the Penns were not as unpopular throughout Pennsylvania as they were with Franklin. His petition against them attracted just 3,500 signatures. Petitions supporting them garnered 15,000. In that fall's bitter election campaign for the Assembly, the illegitimacy of Franklin's son became an issue. He lost his seat.

But he quickly gained a new mission that he was only too glad to assume.

STAMPED TO DEATH *To protest the Stamp Act, the Pennsylvania Journal, its front page festooned with death's head parodies of the tax stamp, suspended publication.*

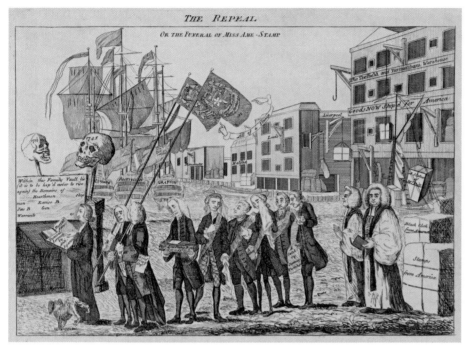

The Assembly voted to submit the petition against the Proprietors to the crown and to send Franklin to London for that purpose. As always, Deborah declined to accompany him. Did she fear that she might prove unsuited to the sophisticated London circles where her husband moved easily? Did he? If they did, neither said so. By November, Franklin was once again ready to board ship for London. Three hundred shouting supporters accompanied him to the pier.

STAMP OF DISAPPROVAL

In London, Franklin headed back at once to Mrs. Stevenson's house on Craven Street. Soon he also brought his 4-year-old grandson, Temple, to live with him, though under the name William Temple, so most people didn't realize he was Franklin's grandson. He had not been in London long before he became embroiled in a new controversy. Because the Seven Years War had severely stressed the British treasury, Britain's ministries were devising schemes to raise revenue. One, called the Sugar Act of 1764, placed a modest duty on molasses imported to the colonies from the French and Spanish West Indies to produce rum. Though it was unpopular in the colonies, Franklin found it unobjectionable. In his view Britain had a right to impose import duties, something different from taxes. He even wrote to a British friend: "You will take care for your own sakes not to lay greater burdens on us than we can bear; for you cannot hurt us without hurting yourselves."

But British Prime Minister George Grenville had another plan—a tax on all kinds of printed matter. Newspapers and almanacs, leases, and other legal documents would all require an official tax stamp. Franklin and other agents for the colonies succeeded in gaining a meeting with Grenville to plead their case that the colonies could be taxed only by their own legislatures. Grenville was unmoved. By March 1765 the Stamp Act was law.

At this point Franklin made one of the worst misjudgments of his political life. He utterly failed to understand the depth of opposition to the tax among the colonists. Though he opposed the Stamp Act and hoped to have it repealed, he was willing to make attempts to accommodate the British. Meanwhile, back home, outrage over the Stamp Act escalated quickly. By spring the Virginia House of Burgesses, egged on by a fiery new member named Patrick Henry, had adopted a series of resolutions asserting that Virginians could be taxed only by their elected representatives. Soon Rhode Island and New York joined suit. All around the colonies groups calling themselves the Sons of Liberty sprouted up to organize resistance to the Stamp Act.

Sometimes the protests turned violent. In August a Boston mob ransacked the homes of the Massachusetts stamp commissioner and the lieutenant governor. In September an unruly crowd in Philadelphia, convinced that Franklin was a keen supporter of the Stamp Act, threatened to level his new house on Market Street. Deborah stood her ground and with the help of armed friends fended off the mob. Franklin wrote to his plucky wife afterward, "I honor much the spirit and courage you showed. The woman deserves a good house that is determined to defend it."

By now he understood that he had made a serious mistake. He would soon embark on a campaign to rescue his reputation through letters and journal articles attacking the Stamp Act, a mission of self-resurrection that culminated in February 1766, when he was called before Parliament to present the colonists' objections to the Act in a lengthy question-and-answer session. A new government headed by Lord Rockingham had replaced Grenville's and was aiming to repeal the hated Act. Franklin was summoned in the hope his arguments would give Rockingham's government a face-saving way out.

ANOTHER FAMILY
In 1767 Franklin's daughter, Sally, would marry Richard Bache, at left. An English immigrant, he would become a shopkeeper in Philadelphia. Below, Sally as she appeared during a trip to England in 1793, where she had her portrait painted by the London artist John Hoppner.

Face saving for him too. His performance was suitably brilliant, though in the course of the day he acknowledged that Britain had a right to impose "external" taxes on the colonies, like import duties, something most Americans were no longer willing to concede. But within a month the Stamp Act had been repealed. And when a verbatim account of Franklin's words before Parliament was circulated around the colonies, his improbable image makeover was complete. The man whose house came near to burning by Stamp Act protesters was being celebrated as the great defender of colonial rights.

A COMPLICATED GAME In the year that followed, Franklin turned his attention more often to personal matters. In the summer Deborah wrote to tell him that their daughter Sally was seeking

On friday Sept. 30th 1768. the ships of WAR, armed Schooners, Transports, &c. Came up the Harbour and Anchored round the Town; their Cannon loaded, a Spring on their Cables, as for a regular Siege. At noon on Saturday October the 1st the fourteenth & twenty-ninth Regiments, a detachment from the 59th Regt. and Train of Artillery, with two pieces of Cannon, landed on the Long Wharf; there Formed and Marched with Insolent Parade, Drums beating, Fifes playing, and Colours flying, up KING STREET. Each Soldier having received 16 rounds of Powder and Ball.

Col: by Ch. Remich

ENGRAVED PRINTED, & SOLD by PAUL REVERE, Boston

UNHAPPY LANDING *A Paul Revere engraving shows the 1768 arrival of British troops in Boston to enforce search-and-seizure laws.*

his approval to marry Richard Bache, an English immigrant who operated a dry-goods store in Philadelphia. He wrote back to say he was not sure he would be able to return from London that summer. "I would not occasion a delay in her happiness if you thought the match a proper one."

How proper soon became an issue, after Franklin's son William checked into the finances of the man proposing to marry his sister and discovered that Bache was in serious debt. In a letter to Sally, Franklin did not explicitly forbid her to marry the man, but he also wrote his wife to say he assumed that Bache would soon be out of the picture. He would be wrong about that—in October, Bache and Sally wed. Franklin, however, would not be there for the ceremony. Nor did he go home that winter when his wife suffered a serious stroke. Nothing it seems, could tempt him home. Yet during the previous summer nothing had prevented him from heading off with a friend, the physician John Pringle, on a trip to Germany, where he could bask in his fame just as he had in Scotland.

Meanwhile, Franklin was also working to further a project he had pursued with mixed success for years—obtaining land grants in North America. Two years earlier he had become one of a group of investors who were jointly awarded 200,000 acres in Nova Scotia by the British government. In the summer of 1767 he joined with his son William in a group hoping to obtain even larger grants west of the Ohio River. More than once that year Franklin dined with Lord Shelburne, who as secretary of

The Ladies' Man

BY CLAUDE-ANNE LOPEZ

From his days as a young printer in Philadelphia to his years as a diplomatic star in France, Franklin surrounded himself with adoring women, often much younger, usually attractive, and preferably intelligent. For the most part, his wife, Deborah, tolerated these dalliances. As she probably knew, most were never consummated. Franklin was a master of what the French call *amitié amoureuse*, a delicious form of intimacy, expressed in exchanges of teasing kisses, tender embraces, intimate conversations, and rhapsodic love letters, but not necessarily sexual congress. A peek inside his not-so-little black book:

Catharine Ray: A Wintry Love

They first meet around Christmastime 1754 while he is inspecting New England's postal network. He is 48 and at the peak of his scientific glory; she is 23, vivacious, opinionated, and uninhibited. Basking in his attentions on a visit to Boston from her home on Block Island, off the Rhode Island coast, Catharine Ray chatters away. She makes him sugar plums, which he pronounces better than any he has ever tasted. A few days later, they set off for Rhode Island. It is a wintry journey marked by "a wrong road and a soaking shower," he later recalls. But they talk for hours on end, mutually smitten. Back in Philadelphia, he responds to her first letter with rhapsody and rue: The northeast wind "is the gaiest wind," he writes, because it brought her promised kisses mingled with snowflakes, as "pure as your virgin innocence, white as your lovely bosom…"

Catharine's ardor rises. "Absence rather increases than lessens my affections," she writes. But by now Franklin senses all this may be going too far, and he retreats to an avuncular tone, advising her to marry and surround herself with "clusters of plump, juicy, blushing, pretty little rogues like their Mama."

And that is just what Catharine does. By their next meeting, she is Mrs. William Greene Jr., wife of Rhode Island's future governor and mother of the first two of their six children. She and Franklin will always remain friends.

Polly Stevenson: A Second Daughter

When Franklin returns to Britain in 1757 as a political agent of the American colonies, he moves into a four-story townhouse near London's busy Strand. Its owner: a solicitous widow named Margaret Stevenson, with whom he may have had an affair during his 15 years under her roof. But Franklin's real interest is her brainy daughter Mary, who goes by the nickname Polly. Only 18 years old when she enters his life, she shows such an eagerness to learn that it stirs all his strong mentoring instincts.

When she leaves London to live with an aunt in the country, they begin an extraordinary correspondence. It covers the full breadth of moral and natural philosophy. Always prim but also refreshingly direct, Polly poses her questions—about barometers, insects, river tides, electrical storms—and he responds in the flattering style he inevitably uses with young women who catch his eye. He ends one dense six-page tract, for example, by musing how he might sign off to so receptive a mind as hers. "I had rather conclude abruptly with what pleases me more than any Compliment can please you, that I am allow'd to subscribe myself Your affectionate Friend."

He imagines, he tells her, a marriage between her and his son William. But William is in love with another woman. Leaving London soon thereafter, Franklin laments how distressed he is at the thought of never seeing Polly again. But

MADAME HELVÉTIUS

POLLY STEVENSON

"Keep your eyes wide
open before marriage,
half shut afterwards."

—BENJAMIN FRANKLIN

he returns two years later, and before long gives her away in marriage to a physician, William Hewson. Sixteen years later, after her husband's death, Franklin finally gets her permanently at his side when she and her three children come to live near him in Philadelphia until he dies.

Mesdames Brillon and Helvétius: Parisian Soul Mates

The lovely and talented Anne-Louise d'Hardancourt Brillon de Jouy plays the harpsichord and piano like an angel. Eager to meet her new neighbor in the fashionable Paris suburb of Passy, she woos him with a recital of Scottish songs. She follows with invitations to tea and chess games in which she pours out her troubled soul to him. The delighted Franklin soon presses her for more tangible evidence of her affection. She plays coy, however, and steers the relationship with "Cher Papa" into a safer daughter-father pattern, over his useless protests.

The Franklin libido really stirs when he encounters Anne-Catherine de Ligniville d'Autricourt, a descendant of Austrian nobility known by her married name, Madame Helvétius. Outgoing and earthy, she uses her late husband's fortune to operate a bohemian estate, filled with animals, on the fringes of the Bois de Boulogne, where she reigns over a salon of Enlightenment philosophers. To Franklin, this is an intellectual heaven.

Franklin proposes marriage to Madame Helvétius but frames the offer so that it can be taken seriously or seen as a joke. He tells her that her late husband and his late Deborah have wed in heaven, so it would be fitting if she accepted him on earth. When he finally returns to America, her friends chide her for not accepting his proposal and keeping the adored Franklin in France. ■

Claude-Anne Lopez is the author of Mon Cher Papa: Franklin and the Ladies of Paris.

DAVID HUME

JAMES BOSWELL

WILLIAM STRAHAN

CIRCLE OF ADMIRERS
His move to London gave Franklin the opportunity to enjoy the company of distinguished friends. Clockwise from lower left, James Boswell would gain fame as the biographer of Samuel Johnson; the Scottish philosopher David Hume was a key figure of the Enlightenment; the printer William Strahan, in a portrait by Joshua Reynolds, would become a member of Parliament.

state for the Southern Department of the American Colonies could approve the grant. Shelburne was sympathetic. But in time his department was absorbed by a larger one, in charge of all colonial affairs, headed by the much less sympathetic Lord Hillsborough, who squashed the plan.

That same summer Franklin would also begin to regret his support for Britain's right to impose customs duties, which merely demonstrated how out of touch he still was with sentiment back home. In June 1767 Charles Townshend, Britain's Chancellor of the Exchequer, asked Parliament to approve duties on a number of British exports to the colonies, including paper, glass, china, paint, and tea. The Townshend duties immediately set off a wave of protests in the colonies and boycotts of British goods. Early the next year the Massachusetts House circulated a letter to the other colonies petitioning for repeal. Franklin responded with articles in the English press that attempted to explain American views on the subject without explicitly endorsing them. But as he confessed in a letter to his son William, he was becoming convinced either that "Parliament has a power to make all laws for us, or that it has the power to make no laws for us."

At the time Franklin was playing a complicated game. There were rumors that he might be appointed undersecretary for colonial affairs, serving under the same Lord Hillsborough who had quashed his land grant scheme. As long as the job remained a possibility, it would not do for Franklin to be too aggressive in denouncing the British position on the powers of colonial assemblies. But in August he had an angry meeting with Hillsborough that ended any job prospect.

TALKFESTS *Franklin enjoyed London coffeehouses like this one, where people gathered to discuss events of the day.*

Meanwhile, the situation at home continued to deteriorate. Lord Hillsborough demanded that the Massachusetts House rescind its letter calling for repeal of the Townshend duties. When the House refused, he sent two regiments of British soldiers to patrol the increasingly uneasy streets of Boston. In March 1770 the inevitable happened. A confrontation between a young Bostonian and a British officer escalated into a mob scene that ended with a group of besieged redcoats firing on the crowd. Five people were killed and six wounded. It would soon be known as the Boston Massacre.

LOCKING HORNS WITH HILLSBOROUGH By coincidence, on the very day of the Boston Massacre, Parliament repealed all of the Townshend duties except for the one on tea, which it left as a way to assert its right to impose tariffs on the colonies. But ever more colonists were rejecting the idea that Parliament had such a power. By now Franklin had arrived at the same position. He still hoped that a way could be found to head off a split with the mother country. But his attempts to mediate were often met with suspicion on both sides. As he put it, he was suspected "in England of being too much an American, and in America of being too much an Englishman." He also still had personal ambitions that obliged him to maintain the goodwill of powerful people in the British government. One was another attempt to gain a large land grant, this time with a group calling itself the Grand Ohio Company—a project that would require the good favor of Lord Hillsborough. And the Duke of Grafton, who headed the Treasury, had hinted that he might be able find Franklin some official post.

THE KILLING FIELDS
An engraving by Paul Revere depicts British soldiers opening fire on Americans during the Boston Massacre of March 5, 1770.

But then came yet another disastrous meeting between Franklin and Hillsborough. Early in 1771 he came to Hillsborough's home to inform him that the Massachusetts House of Representatives had appointed him to serve as its agent in England. But no sooner had Franklin gotten out those words than Hillsborough, with, as Franklin would later write, "something between a smile and a sneer," interrupted him to say that he could not be appointed agent without the agreement of the royal governor of Massachusetts. Franklin disputed him, explaining that as agent he represented the people, who had the right to choose whomever they pleased without the governor's approval, an argument that caused Hillsborough to assume "a mixed look of anger and contempt." Franklin had no less contempt for Hillsborough. But in time he would realize to his own dismay that Hillsborough's narrow view of colonial prerogatives had the support of his government.

By the summer, Franklin sought to cheer himself by his customary means, a season of travels. It was during one of them, while staying at the country house of a friend, the Anglican Bishop Jonathan Shipley, that the 65-year-old Franklin embarked on his *Autobiography*. He framed the text as a letter to his son William, though it's plain that he was also speaking to a wider audience. His purpose was to remind both his son and the larger public that though Benjamin Franklin had risen far in the world, he had sprung from humble origins. Franklin worked steadily on the book for three weeks, reading aloud in the evening to the Shipleys the portions he had written that day. He brought his story up to 1731 and his founding of the lending library, then put the project aside. It would be 13 years before he would return to it.

THE BOSTON TEA PARTY
To protest actions by Parliament to control the tea trade, on Dec. 16, 1773, a group of colonists dressed as Indians threw 342 chests of British tea into Boston Harbor.

Franklin continued his travels through Ireland and Scotland. In Ireland he was surprised to find himself for almost a week the invited houseguest of none other than Lord Hillsborough, who showed him no end of warmth and consideration. Franklin suspected that Hillsborough had some ulterior motive, but was not sure what. His suspicions only heightened after he returned to London. When he attempted to call on Hillsborough at home to thank him for his hospitality, he was repeatedly told that the master was not at home, when he plainly was.

That summer Franklin also for the first time met his son-in-law, Richard Bache, who was visiting London in the hope of getting a public appointment of some kind. Thoroughly wary by now of the public appointment game, Franklin advised Bache to go home and start a business. But he wrote back to wife Deborah to say he approved of Bache. If nothing else, the man had sired Franklin's first legitimate grandchild. Benjamin Franklin Bache, called Benny, had been born two years earlier.

The following June, Franklin would also have a sweet revenge against Hillsborough. For almost two years Hillsborough had succeeded in delaying action on the land grant sought by the Grand Ohio Company. But some powerful men were partners in that venture, including Thomas and Richard Walpole, nephews of former Prime Minister Robert Walpole. They succeeded in pushing the matter forward to the Board of Trade, the body governing colonial affairs that was headed by Hillsborough. Though the board recommended against the request, the final decision rested with the king's Privy

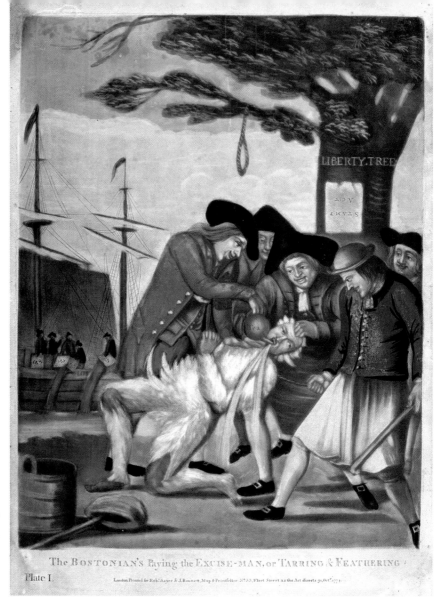

The BOSTONIAN'S Paying the EXCISE-MAN, or TARRING & FEATHERING

Plate I.

London Printed for Rob.ᵗ Sayer & J. Bennett, Map & Printseller, N.º53, Fleet Street, as the Act directs 30 Oct.ʳ 1774.

ROUGH JUSTICE
A British print shows a scene of John Malcolm, Boston's Commissioner of Customs, being tarred and feathered by colonists, with the Boston Tea Party, an earlier event, in the background.

Council. When the Council met, Hillsborough made the serious blunder of threatening to resign his post if the grant was approved. It was, and he did.

The partnership would never get its land—relations between Britain and her colonies would reach the crisis stage before that could happen. But Franklin had the satisfaction of seeing Hillsborough go. His replacement, Lord Dartmouth, had no problem with accepting Franklin as agent for Massachusetts, even without the royal governor's approval. Franklin wrote happily to his friend Thomas Cushing, the Massachusetts Speaker of the House, "I hope business is getting into better train."

INTO THE COCKPIT With the genial Lord Dartmouth as head of American affairs, Franklin was more optimistic about relations between Britain and her colonies. In the hope of improving them he took a step that would embroil him in one of the greatest controversies of his career. In December 1772 he sent Thomas Cushing, the Massachusetts House Speaker, a packet of letters that had come into his possession—he would never explain how. Many were written in the late 1760s by Thomas Hutchinson, then lieutenant governor of Massachusetts, and his brother-in-law Andrew Oliver. The recipient had been Thomas Whately, a British undersecretary. What they amounted to was a plea from two prominent men of Massachusetts for Britain to crack down on their own unruly colony.

Hutchinson in particular argued that Britain must use firm measures to curtail the rising unrest in the colonies. "An abridgment of what are called English liberties" was necessary, he wrote. Though Franklin told Cushing not to publish the letters, he urged him to show them to other "men of worth." His aim was to convince people in Massachusetts that British attempts to subjugate them did not stem from ill will toward Americans but instead were prompted by bad advice from a few misguided colonial officials. Inevitably the letters went public. By the following year they had been published in a pamphlet that was read all over Massachusetts. But rather than interpret the letters in the way Franklin had hoped, the Massachusetts colonists saw them as evidence of collusion between the crown and its agents in Massachusetts to deprive Americans of their liberties. Indignant members of the Massachusetts House of Representatives petitioned the crown to recall Hutchinson and Oliver.

By August the letters had been published in England as well. When Franklin acknowledged that it was he who had sent them to Massachusetts, it set off a hail of questions about how he had obtained them and an angry campaign against him in the British press. Then, in mid-December, came the Boston Tea Party. To protest a decision by Parliament to give the East India Company a virtual monopoly over tea imports to the colonies, some 50 patriots disguised as Indians dumped 90,000 pounds of British tea into Boston Harbor. News of the incident inflamed feeling in Britain further.

Events reached a crescendo on Jan. 29, 1774, when Franklin appeared before the king's Privy Council in an amphitheater in Whitehall called "the Cockpit." Facing a packed house of spectators that included Franklin's nemesis, Lord Hillsborough, he listened to a storm of angry questions as to how he had obtained the Hutchinson letters. Franklin would later compare the session to a "bull baiting." For nearly an hour Britain's acid-tongued solicitor general, Alexander Wedderburn, abused and berated Franklin, even calling him a thief. By making public what was intended to be a private

"A great empire, like a great cake, is most easily diminished at the edges." —BENJAMIN FRANKLIN, *Rules by Which a Great Empire May Be Reduced to a Small One*

AN EARLY STEP TOWARD UNITY

In September 1774, while Franklin was still in London, the colonies convened the first Continental Congress in Philadelphia to respond to British reprisals for the Boston Tea Party, which included closing Boston Harbor. At left, delegates pray on opening day. The Congress met in Carpenters' Hall, above, which was also the home of Franklin's Library Company and his American Philosophical Society.

THE COCKPIT
*A silent Franklin endures his painful
appearance before the king's Privy Council.*

BACK-CHANNEL DIPLOMATS
Late in 1774 former Prime Minister William Pitt, above, and British admiral Lord Richard Howe, at right, made a quiet attempt to collaborate with Franklin on a plan to avert a split between Britain and her colonies. But when their outline of a compromise was presented before the House of Lords, it was rejected.

correspondence, Wedderburn told the jeering crowd, Franklin had "forfeited all the respect of societies and of men." Wearing a velvet suit, Franklin stood silent and motionless throughout the lengthy dressing-down, then refused to offer any defense of himself.

At the close of the boisterous session, the Privy Council rejected the Massachusetts petition. One day later Franklin was removed from his job as deputy postmaster for the colonies. With his influence in England now at low ebb, many people expected him to return at last to America. Instead he lingered on Craven Street, publishing satires of British policy in the London press and defenses of himself under assumed names, and writing letters in support of plans for a Continental Congress in September to which all the colonies would send representatives. He hoped it would vote for a colony-wide boycott of British goods, the very step it took when it convened in Philadelphia.

Franklin would still be in London when his wife, Deborah, died in December. William wrote to tell him the news, adding pointedly, "I heartily wish you had happened to have come over in the fall, as I think her disappointment preyed a good deal on her spirits." But by that time Franklin was already caught up in one final episode of intrigue. In the summer he had been invited to pay a visit to Lord Chatham, formerly William Pitt the Elder, who had served two terms as one of Britain's most formidable Prime Ministers. A strong supporter of the American colonies, he was also one of the architects of the British Empire, and was concerned that his work was coming undone. Not long after, Franklin received an invitation to play chess with Caroline Howe, a wealthy London matron who was the sister of two important British military officers, Adm. Richard Howe and Gen. William Howe. More than chess would be involved. At their second meeting Mrs. Howe suggested that Franklin might yet serve as an agent to reconcile Britain and the colonies. At their next game she produced

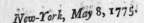

New-York, May 8, 1775.

Extract of a Letter From Philadelphia,

To a Gentleman in this City, dated the 6th inst.

YESTERDAY evening Dr. FRANKLIN arrived here from London in six weeks, which he left the 20th of March, which has given great joy to this town, he says we have no favours to expect from the Ministry, nothing but submission will satisfy them, they expect little or no opposition will be made to their troops, those that are now coming are for *New-York*, where it is expected they will be received with cordiality. As near as we can learn there are about four thousand troops coming in this fleet, the men of war and transports are in a great measure loaded with dry goods, to supply *New-York*, and the country round it, agents are coming over with them. Dr. *Franklin* is highly pleased to find us arming and preparing for the worst events, he thinks nothing else can save us from the most abject slavery and destruction, at the same time encourages us to believe a spirited opposition, will be the means of our salvation. The Ministry are alarmed at every opposition, and lifted up again at every thing which appears the least in their favour, every letter and every paper from hence, are read by them.

N E W - Y O R K:
Printed by JOHN ANDERSON, at Beckman's-Slip.

THE GREAT MAN SPEAKS
On his return to Philadelphia, Franklin was interviewed for a press account that appeared as a published letter.

her brother Richard, who hinted to Franklin that at least some ministers in the British government were still hoping it was possible to come to terms with the colonies. Next it was Chatham who came back to Franklin, conferring with him several times on a plan to address the colonists' grievances on terms Britain could also accept.

But all hopes were in vain, as Franklin would learn in February when he would accompany Chatham to Parliament to watch him introduce the plan in the House of Lords. It was rejected out of hand, but not before Lord Sandwich, First Lord of the Admiralty, rose to declare that the proposals could not have been drafted by an Englishman and must be the work of an American. Looking directly at Franklin, who was sitting in the gallery, he announced that they must be the work of "one of the bitterest and most mischievous enemies this country has ever known."

Franklin's usefulness as a mediator was clearly over. It was time at last to leave England. In March, with 15-year-old Temple in tow, he boarded a ship for home. ∎

85

THE REBEL
AND THE
DIPLOMAT

E ven before Franklin arrived in Philadelphia, the situation in the colonies took another fateful turn. On the night of April 18, 1775, a detachment of British soldiers stationed in Boston set out for nearby Concord to seize a cache of weapons stockpiled by patriot militias. Paul Revere got word of the scheme and set off on horseback to alert the countryside with a cry that would ring down through the centuries: "The redcoats are coming!"

Revere reached Lexington in time to warn the patriots Sam Adams and John Hancock before they could be arrested. When the British contingent arrived at daybreak, about 70 American "minutemen" had mustered to confront them. Shots were fired. In the ensuing fight, eight Americans were killed and 10 wounded. The redcoats suffered barely a scrape.

From there they pressed on to Concord, where this time a larger group of militia had assembled. Now it was the redcoats who would bleed. Harried by the American fighters, they turned back toward Boston, but in the long day's march they were fired upon regularly by snipers in the woods and militiamen in hot pursuit. By nightfall they had suffered as many as 270 dead and wounded.

This was no longer a squabble between Britain and its colonies. It was war,

THE WAR EXPANDS
On June 17, 1775, during the Battle of Bunker Hill, near Boston, British troops burned Charlestown to the ground.

BOSTON

View of The
Burnin

CHARLES TOWN

TTACK *on* BUNKER's HILL, *with the*
of CHARLES TOWN, *June 17, 1775.*

Drawn by Earl & engraved by A.Doolittle in 1775   Re-Engraved by A.Doolittle and J.N

BATTLE OF LEXINGTON.

1. *Major Pitcairn at the head of the Regular Granadiers.—*2. *The Party who first fired on the Provincia* 3.*Part of the Provincial Company of Lexington.—*4. *Regular Companies on the road to Concord.—*5. *The at Lexington.—*6. *The Public Inn.*

THE SHOT HEARD AROUND THE WORLD *The first battle of the Revolutionary War was the deadly skirmish at Lexington, Mass.*

and in response to the blunt escalation of hostilities the Continental Congress that had met the year before decided to reconvene. When Franklin disembarked in Philadelphia on May 5, Thomas Jefferson, John Adams, Hancock, and Patrick Henry were already converging upon Philadelphia. Within a day he was chosen by the Pennsylvania Assembly to join them as a delegate. Nearly 70, he would be by far the oldest man in attendance.

Franklin was so quiet during much of the Congress that some delegates suspected him of being a spy for the British. It didn't help that unlike most of them, who had come to Philadelphia from other towns, he did not socialize at the inns and taverns at night. Instead he went home to the house on Market Street that he had built for his late wife but had never seen, to the company of his daughter, Sally, her husband, Richard, and their sons, Benny and now also William. But when Franklin did speak out, any suspicions about his loyalty fell away. Still feeling the sting of his personal humiliation in London, he would prove to be one of the delegates most determined to see the colonies break away from England, an outcome many others were still unwilling to entertain.

It was probably not a good portent for Franklin's future relations with his son that the old man did not bother to inform William that he was coming back to America. The royal governor of New

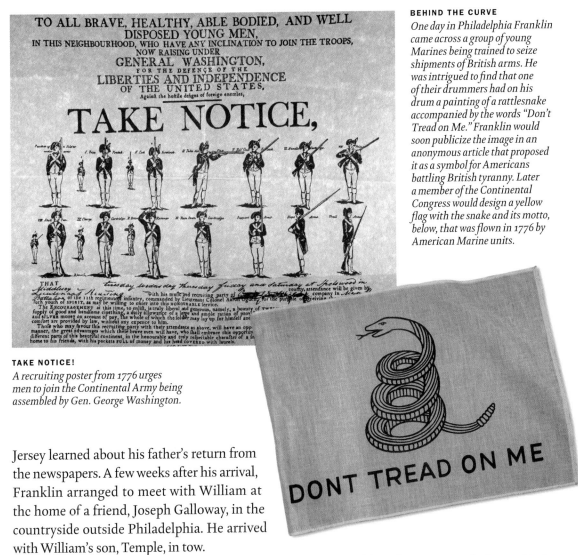

TAKE NOTICE!

A recruiting poster from 1776 urges
men to join the Continental Army being
assembled by Gen. George Washington.

Jersey learned about his father's return from the newspapers. A few weeks after his arrival, Franklin arranged to meet with William at the home of a friend, Joseph Galloway, in the countryside outside Philadelphia. He arrived with William's son, Temple, in tow.

Inevitably the reunion produced an argument between Franklin, who passionately favored independence, and William, a servant of the crown. But at the end of the evening Franklin handed over Temple, who would spend the summer with his father.

With June came the battle of Bunker Hill, outside Boston, during which British forces burned Charlestown, Mass., to the ground. With the war growing fiercer all the time, colonial unity seemed more essential to Franklin than ever. To promote it he drew up a proposal for a new government modeled on the Albany plan he had developed two decades earlier, but with an even more powerful central authority to handle foreign affairs, oversee defense, settle disputes among the colonies, handle relations with Indian tribes, and issue a common currency. His Articles of Confederation, as he called his plan, provided for a congress with a single chamber in which each colony would be represented proportionally in accordance with its population. There would not be a president. Instead, the executive would be a council in which members would serve staggered three-year terms.

Franklin understood perfectly well that this was a scheme beyond anything the Continental Congress was prepared to endorse. So he merely read his text to a committee of the whole Congress, not insisting on a vote. Then he waited for history to catch up with him.

AGENT OF THE CONTINENTAL CONGRESS To Franklin's satisfaction, the Continental Congress voted unanimously to make him postmaster general of the American colonies. Though he donated his salary to care for wounded soldiers, he also made sure to appoint his son-in-law, Richard Bache, the postal system's chief financial officer. That fall Franklin was also part of a mission from the Congress that traveled to Boston to meet with Gen. Washington, who was attempting to cobble together a real army from the ragtag Massachusetts militia and sundry volunteers from other colonies. While there Franklin drew up a detailed list of measures for soldiers' rations and military discipline—a minimum of 20 lashes, for instance, for any sentry caught sleeping. As they were leaving, Washington emphasized to the congressional envoys the need for regular funding from the Congress. With his typical practicality, Franklin wrote later to Bache that if the cost of the Army was £1.2 million a year, that sum could be raised "if 500,000 families will each spend a shilling a week less."

By March, Franklin had been dispatched by the Congress on another mission, this time to Canada, as head of a delegation sent to determine whether to send reinforcements to assist Gen. Benedict Arnold. A few months earlier American forces led in part by Arnold had failed, disastrously, in an attempt to take Quebec from the British. With virtually no financial support from the Congress, the surviving Americans had regrouped to spend a miserable winter living off the land of increasingly resentful Canadians, who were wondering if they would ever be paid.

The journey north was so difficult for Franklin's group that at one stop along the way he wrote to his friend Josiah Quincy that "I have undertaken a fatigue that at my time of life may prove too much for me. So I sit down to write to a few friends by way of farewell." In fact he would survive to reach Montreal and complete his mission, which ended with the delegation concluding that it was best to withdraw American troops from Canada altogether if the Congress could not afford to support them. Sick and exhausted, Franklin returned to Philadelphia in May.

"However strange it may appear to some…nothing can settle our affairs so expeditiously as an open and determined declaration for independence."

— THOMAS PAINE,
from Common Sense

LITTLE BOOKLET, BIG IMPACT
Common Sense, *the pamphlet by Tom Paine, far right, was only 47 pages long, but it had a powerful effect in legitimizing the goal of independence.*

ARRESTED DEVELOPMENT *A British royal governor, Franklin's son was seized in 1776 and sent to prison.*

DECLARING INDEPENDENCE By the time Franklin returned to Philadelphia, there had been a great change in public opinion on the topic of independence. For as long as they could, the rebellious colonists had sustained the hope that they could resolve their differences with Britain and remain a part of its empire. But the prolonged shooting war made that harder to imagine. Then, in January, a pamphlet from someone who signed himself simply "an Englishman" electrified the colonies with a powerful argument that independence was both desirable and inevitable.

Within a few weeks after it first appeared in Philadelphia, *Common Sense*, as the 47-page pamphlet was called, sold a phenomenal 120,000 copies—this at a time when the English colonies had a non-slave population of only around 2 million. Eventually it would emerge that its author was a Quaker émigré from England, Thomas Paine, a former corset maker, schoolteacher, and tax collector who had arrived in Philadelphia in 1774. There he found his true calling as a kind of crusading journalist, denouncing the slave trade and promoting a plan of pensions for the elderly.

Even before coming to Pennsylvania, Paine had a close connection to Franklin. In London, where Paine had sought him out, Franklin found himself charmed by this fellow who, like him, had a working knowledge of many fields and was unimpressed by British claims of authority. When Paine told Franklin that he would like to immigrate to America, Franklin supplied him with a letter of introduction to his son-in-law, asking Bache to help Paine find employment. Later Paine showed the manuscript of *Common Sense* to Franklin, who offered a few suggestions and urged him on.

Paine's pamphlet, with its ringing conclusion that "a government of our own is our natural right," helped tilt colonial opinion in favor of independence. On June 7 a Virginia delegate to the Congress, Richard Henry Lee, put forward a motion "that these United Colonies are, and of right ought to be, free and independent states." The Congress decided to postpone a vote until July 2. But as a first step it called for the removal of all royal governments. So it was that within a week, a new provincial legislature in New Jersey ordered the arrest of Gov. William Franklin. Mindful that his father was a famous patriot, the legislature asked that his arrest be handled "with all the delicacy and tenderness which the nature of the business can possibly admit." Franklin did not lift a finger to help his son. When William was put on trial on June 21, his father did not attend. When the Congress voted three days later to send him to prison in Connecticut, Franklin kept out of it. Later he did see fit to send money to William's wife. But he would also forbid Temple from visiting his father in prison.

Meanwhile he had important work to do. The Congress had decided to appoint a committee to draft a statement setting out its reasons for declaring independence. With Thomas Jefferson of Virginia as its chairman, the committee included John Adams of Massachusetts, Robert Livingston of New York, Roger Sherman of Connecticut, and Franklin. Most of the work of drafting this Declaration of Independence would fall to Jefferson, who labored over his text in a second-story room not far from Franklin's house on Market Street.

When Jefferson completed his draft, he sent it over to Franklin to suggest changes. Recognizing the power of Jefferson's words, Franklin changed very little, though one of his edits would ring down through the ages. Where Jefferson had written "We hold these truths to be sacred and undeniable," Franklin substituted the almost literally immortal words "We hold these truths to be self-evident."

At the official signing of the Declaration in August, John Hancock, the president of the Congress, announced: "There must be no pulling different ways. We must all hang together." According to Jared Sparks, a 19th-century historian, Franklin made a now famous reply: "Yes, we must, indeed, all hang together, or most assuredly we shall all hang separately."

Above, the committee that drafted the Declaration of Independence presents the finished document to John Hancock, president of the Continental Congress. In the foreground Franklin can be seen seated in profile. At left, a page from Jefferson's handwritten draft shows Franklin's changes and additions.

CREATING A NEW NATION A 70-year-old man afflicted with gout and kidney stones, Franklin was energized by the great developments of that summer. No sooner had he finished the work of the Declaration than he was named president of the convention drafting a new constitution for what was now the state of Pennsylvania. Fortunately, it was meeting in the same building as the Continental Congress, where Franklin was already collaborating with the other delegates to invent the form that the new national government would take.

Franklin spent the summer going back and forth between the two convocations. In both he pressed for an institutional structure along the lines he had proposed in his Articles of Confederation the year before. In particular he favored the idea of a legislature with a single chamber, with each state represented in proportion to its population. In the Continental Congress, where each former colony was jealous of its sovereignty and where the smaller ones feared being overwhelmed by the larger, proportional representation was a highly combustible topic. Inevitably the idea was rejected in favor of a legislature in which each state, no matter what its population, would have one vote.

Franklin had more success in persuading the Pennsylvania state convention to reject the idea of a legislature with two chambers, one with representatives elected directly by the people, the other an "upper" chamber chosen by other means. To many people the advantage of an upper chamber, whose members were likely to come from men of property, was the restraint it could impose on the people's

Franklin in Passy

In the summer of 1785, as he was preparing to make a reluctant return to Philadelphia, Franklin would describe France as "the country that I love the most in the world." Certainly life had been sweet for him there. Very soon after his arrival in 1776 he had moved to Passy, a village just outside Paris and conveniently on the road to the court at Versailles. There he would live as a guest on the estate of Jacques-Donatien Leray de Chaumont, a wealthy merchant who installed Franklin in a fine house with a garden and vowed not to accept rent until America had triumphed in its struggle for independence.

Franklin would be hugely popular in France. As John Adams would recall: "There was scarcely a peasant or a citizen, a valet de chambre, coachman or footman, a lady's chambermaid or a scullion in the kitchen who was not familiar with Franklin's name." His likeness in the form of prints, busts, and medallions was so widespread that, as he wrote to his daughter Sally, they "have made your father's face as well known as that of the moon."

During his years in France, Franklin would also be witness to the last sumptuous moments of the Old Regime, a world of wealth and privilege that would be swept away by the French Revolution in 1789.

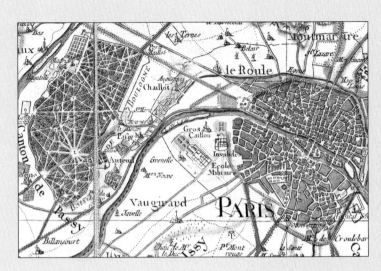

TOWN & COUNTRY
An 18th-century map of Paris and its environs shows Passy to the west of the city, adjacent to the Bois de Boulogne. Below, a panoramic view of Passy as it appeared around 1740 includes in the background a glimpse of Chaumont's villa, with its two triangular green roofs.

> "Tyranny is so…established in the rest of the world that the prospect of an asylum in America for those who love liberty gives general joy."
>
> — BENJAMIN FRANKLIN, *on why America had become "the cause of all mankind"*

THREE'S COMPANY
An engraving on a snuffbox produced after Franklin's death in 1790 depicts him as part of a triumvirate with two French intellectual heroes and champions of liberty, Voltaire and Rousseau.

chamber below. But to Franklin that smacked of the aristocratic presumptions of the British House of Lords. Swayed by his arguments, Pennsylvania would be almost alone among the new states in opting for a single chamber.

In that busy summer, Franklin was also drafted into a diplomatic mission. In mid-July he received a letter from Adm. Lord Richard Howe, who had worked with him in London to find a solution to Britain's dispute with its colonies, and who was now commander of British forces in America. Howe wrote that he and his brother Gen. William Howe were authorized to offer a truce, amnesty for leaders of the rebellion, and rewards for anyone who helped to restore order. The Congress authorized Franklin to reply, which he did in an impassioned letter that detailed for Howe his government's "wanton barbarity and cruelty" in the colonies. As for peace talks, if these were to take place at all, then Britain would have to negotiate with America as a sovereign nation.

PUBLIC PROFILE
Another token of Franklin's popularity in France, a medallion produced there in 1777, the year of his arrival

Howe decided to delay a reply to Franklin's letter. But a few weeks later the Americans suffered a major defeat at the hands of the British in the Battle of Long Island. Hoping that setback might soften the resistance to talks, Howe asked the Congress to send a delegation to meet with him in September. Soon Franklin, John Adams, and Edward Rutledge, all signers of the Declaration, were on their way to join Howe on Staten Island.

The meeting would end in failure. Though Howe promised that Britain was prepared to restore to the colonies the power to control their own laws and taxes—an offer they might eagerly have accepted even a year before—it was now too late for Americans to resume loyalty to the British crown. But if prosecuting the war further was the only alternative, America would need allies, and the most likely partner was Britain's perennial antagonist, France. Less than two weeks after his talks with

COMTE DE VERGENNES

EDWARD BANCROFT

ARTHUR LEE

PARISIAN INTRIGUE
The Comte de Vergennes, at far left, foreign minister of France, was Franklin's main negotiating partner in the delicate dealings to conclude an alliance. Edward Bancroft, the trusted secretary to the American delegation, was secretly a spy for Britain, sending to London regular reports in invisible ink on the progress of Franklin's talks with Vergennes and other matters. Arthur Lee, also an American delegate to France, was Franklin's perennial antagonist—angry, accusatory, and suspicious.

Howe, Franklin was chosen by the Congress to go to France with two other envoys to attempt to conclude an alliance. By October, Franklin was once again aboard a ship crossing the Atlantic.

This time he had his grandsons in tow: Benny was now 7; Temple, about 17. Franklin had not bothered to inform the imprisoned William that he was taking his son to France. Nor did he seek the permission of William's wife, Elizabeth, who was living miserably on her own back in New Jersey. A few months earlier he had refused her request to take some action to allow William to come home to her. Within a year she would be dead, having never seen her husband again.

THE FRENCH CONNECTION If the voyage was hard for Franklin—it "almost demolished" him, he later recalled—the welcome shown by France more than made up for it. The French loved his homespun manner, his bald head, and his fur hat, which inspired French women to adopt wigs that resembled it. But they also took the famous scientist, statesman, and philosopher seriously. As Walter Isaacson says in his excellent biography *Benjamin Franklin: An American Life*, to the French, Franklin was "a symbol both of the virtuous frontier freedom romanticized by Rousseau and of the Enlightenment's reasoned wisdom championed by Voltaire."

Soon Franklin was settled in Passy, halfway between Paris and Versailles, as a guest of Jacques-Donatien Leray de Chaumont, a wealthy merchant sympathetic to America's cause (and hoping to enter its markets). Chaumont provided a house and garden on the grounds of his estate, a place where Franklin could meet with his fellow philosophers, hold court for an entourage of daily visitors, flirt with his retinue of adoring women friends—and plot his campaign to woo France.

In that effort Franklin's principal target would be the French foreign minister, the Comte de Vergennes. Thoroughly anti-British, Vergennes was inclined to aid the Americans, if only because it would weaken Britain to lose its colonies. But the French treasury was already burdened, and a program to build its navy to a strength rivaling Britain's was still two years from completion. War with Britain now—if that's what alliance with America would lead to—would be premature. For that reason

MISSION ACCOMPLISHED *The 1778 Treaty of Alliance between France and America*

PUB. BY JOHN SMITH, 756 SOUTH 4TH ST PHILA.

FRAN

THE AFTERPARTY
At Versailles after the treaty signings, Franklin is crowned with a laurel wreath. A seated Louis XVI and Marie Antoinette look on.

the French were reluctant even to make public their contacts with the Americans. What's more, Louis XVI was unenthusiastic about the whole idea of helping rebels challenge the authority of any king, even the King of England.

So it was at a secret meeting in 1776 that Vergennes asked Franklin to draft a memo summarizing the situation in America. What Franklin came back to him with was a text that adroitly played on French ambitions and fears. If France (and Spain) came to America's aid, he wrote, Britain would probably lose—perhaps to them—its profitable island possessions in the West Indies. On the other hand, if America didn't get help, it might have to end the war, and with it any opportunity for France to benefit from Britain's difficulties.

Franklin's dealings with the two other American envoys in Paris were almost as complex as his talks with Vergennes. Silas Deane of Connecticut was someone he could work with, even if Deane did have a way of lining his own pockets while he served the American cause. Arthur Lee of Virginia was another matter: vengeful, prickly, ever suspicious that Franklin was soft on the French or collaborating with Deane in financial chicanery. In at least some of his suspicions Lee was right. He was right about Edward Bancroft, the trusted secretary of the American delegation. Lee believed Bancroft might be a spy for the British, something later historians would confirm. For years Bancroft conveyed information back to London, sometimes in invisible ink, disclosing details of the talks with the French and other sensitive matters.

By October 1777 America was able to celebrate a significant battlefield victory—the surrender of a large British force at Saratoga, N.Y. Here at last was a triumph that should convince the French that it was a good bet to ally with the Americans. But still they hesitated. Though he strongly opposed ending

N'S RECEPTION AT THE COURT OF FRANCE, 1778.

RESPECTFULLY DEDICATED TO THE PEOPLE OF THE UNITED STATES.

the war with Britain on any terms short of full independence, Franklin knew that to spur the French he might have to play the British card. So the following January he met with a British emissary. Their conversation came to nothing. Franklin spent much of the time venting about English brutality in the colonies (and his own humiliations in London). But he knew the French would hear of the meeting and worry that the Americans were open to a peace with Britain from which France gained nothing.

He was right. In February the French agreed to two treaties, a commercial agreement and a military alliance. It was one of the great triumphs of American diplomacy, and it was largely Franklin's doing. At the signing ceremony he pointedly wore the same velvet suit he had worn years earlier during his ordeal in the Cockpit. For Franklin that day was not just a victory for America. It was a personal vindication.   ■

1778-1785

WINNING THE WAR, MAKING THE PEACE

One of the most complex and fraught relationships in Franklin's later life was with John Adams, the Massachusetts patriot, co-signer of the Declaration, and future President. No sooner had the American treaties with France been signed than the 42-year-old Adams turned up as a newly appointed American envoy to France, replacing Silas Deane, who had been called home to face an embezzlement inquiry. The moralizing Adams was immediately offended by Franklin's way of life in France—his late waking hours, the audiences of admirers who awaited him daily at Passy, the constant dinners and concerts at night, and the near-scandalous flirtations with women like Madame Brillon, whose husband looked on in amusement while he dallied with his own mistress. As Adams put it in his memoirs: "The life of Dr. Franklin was a scene of continual dissipation."

It also galled Adams that Franklin was so widely considered among the French to be the greatest American statesman. As he complained years later to the Philadelphia patriot Benjamin Rush, future accounts of the history of the American Revolution were destined to be a vast distortion, one in which "Dr. Franklin's electrical rod smote the Earth and out sprung General Washington."

JOHN PAUL JONES AND THE *BONHOMME RICHARD* By the fall of 1778 the tensions and rivalries among Franklin, Adams, and the truculent Arthur Lee had become unmanageable. It was time for the Continental Congress to appoint one supreme representative to France, a minister plenipotentiary. At the urging of the French, it chose Franklin, a step that of course infuriated Lee, who embarked on a campaign of letters home to blacken Franklin's reputation. Even for Adams, who had recommended that the post go to Franklin, the appointment was a painful development. He decided it was time to return to Massachusetts.

AT EASE
This relaxed portrait of Franklin, in informal dress, was painted by Anne-Rosalie Filleul, an artist and neighbor of Franklin's during his years at Passy.

100

Adams departed France just as one of the most audacious episodes of the Revolutionary War was getting under way. The headstrong naval commander John Paul Jones was about to launch a campaign against the English fleet. (Adams would be caught up indirectly in that episode when the first ship that was supposed to take him home was drafted into Jones's fleet.) Franklin was very much involved in the Jones expedition, an involvement that grew out of his connection with the Marquis de Lafayette, the young French spitfire who had gone to America to fight gallantly for the cause of liberty and personal glory. During his years in Paris, Franklin was often approached by Europeans seeking his help to gain commissions in the American Army, sometimes from reasons of genuine sympathy with the Americans, sometimes because they were freelance soldiers looking for a job. Franklin gave an assist to a few who would become important friends of the American cause, including the Polish count Casimir Pulaski, who would organize the Continental cavalry, and Baron Friedrich Wilhelm von Steuben, who would introduce the colonials to rigorous Prussian discipline.

But his most fateful sponsorship would be the Marquis. With a letter of introduction from Franklin, Lafayette arrived in America in 1777 and persuaded the Continental Congress to make him a major general. He was 19. Attached to the staff of Gen. Washington, with whom he developed something of a father-son relationship, he was wounded in battle and shared the hardships that winter at Valley Forge. When he learned that France was entering the war on America's side, he returned home hoping to lead the French land forces he expected would soon be heading across the Atlantic. Once there he proposed to Franklin a daring idea. Why not attack England itself? Would it not be a simple matter to raid towns along Britain's largely unprotected seaboard?

Franklin was intrigued. But a campaign of that kind would require a sea commander who knew the coasts. Franklin had just the man. John Paul Jones had begun life simply as John Paul. The son of a Scottish gardener, by age 13 he was already at sea. After doing time as first mate on a slave ship

JOHN ADAMS
During his time as an American envoy to France, the future President was exasperated by the esteem that Franklin enjoyed among the French.

RIDE 'EM IF YOU CAN
A British cartoon depicts King George III being thrown from a bucking horse labeled "America."

he gained command of his own merchant vessel and proved to be the sort of captain who didn't hesitate to wield the lash. One day he flogged the ship's carpenter so brutally the man later died. Murder charges were brought and dropped. Then on another vessel he killed a crewman who challenged his authority. At that point he prudently fled to Virginia and added Jones to his name. When the Revolution began, he threw in his lot with the Americans and made a name conducting the sort of coastal raids against English and Scottish towns that Franklin had in mind.

VICTORY AT SEA *The battle between the* Bonhomme Richard *and the British ship* Serapis. *This 18th-century image was designed for a special optical device that would make it appear in 3-D and would reverse the backward type at top.*

Franklin brought Jones into Lafayette's scheme and helped get him a French ship, the *Duras*. In Franklin's honor, Jones rechristened it the *Bonhomme Richard*—the French rendering of Poor Richard. The idea of a land invasion of England was eventually abandoned, but Jones was left free to harass the British navy. In September 1779 he would lead his ship into one of the most celebrated naval engagements of all time, against the bigger, more heavily armed British warship the *Serapis*. After the *Bonhomme Richard* had suffered severe damage from the enemy's cannons, Jones was challenged by the British captain to surrender. It was then that he is purported to have said—it was in an account not set down until years later—"I have not yet begun to fight!"

What we know for certain is that he had not. Jones rammed the *Serapis* and lashed the two ships together. During three hours of close fighting some of his men climbed the *Serapis*'s masts to throw grenades into its ammunition hold, setting off a huge explosion. The British captain surrendered.

THE PLAN

or a Scene in the French Cabinet Sep.ᵗ 1779

INTRIGUES AND VICTORY John Adams did not remain long in America. By February 1780 he was back in Paris, charged by the Congress to be the American negotiator with Britain when the time came to hammer out a peace treaty. When that might be was still anybody's guess, but all through that year the war would go badly for the Americans.

In May the British general Henry Clinton captured Charleston, S.C., the only real city in the South. Then in the fall it emerged that the American general Benedict Arnold, resentful over having been passed over for promotion by the Congress, had gone over to the British side. His first treacheries dated to the year before, when he began selling Gen. Clinton information on the movements of American troops and French ships. When the unsuspecting Americans made Arnold commander of the American fort at West Point, he secretly offered to deliver it to Clinton. Though the plot was foiled, he escaped to British-held New York City and was made a brigadier general in the British army. By winter American forces were also so badly provisioned that they mutinied twice. To Franklin it appeared that the only hope was to seek more financial aid from the French. He believed passionately that America must hold on until it could achieve some decisive military victory in the war. His fear was that an exhausted Congress would respond to British peace feelers and conclude the war on terms that left America less than fully independent.

THE MAN WITH A PLAN
A British cartoon shows Franklin holding the French court by their noses while he offers a "plan" he never had to drain "the British Ocean" before an invasion by France.

104

"I have passed my 75th year, and I find that the long and severe fit of the gout which I had last winter has shaken me exceedingly."

—FRANKLIN, *in a failed request in 1771 to retire as U.S. representative to France*

In all of this Franklin still saw the French as essential allies—much more than Adams was inclined to do. Franklin was full of gratitude to the nation that had taken him to its heart (and vice versa). Adams, who had never been comfortable among the French, felt that France was supporting America out of pure self-interest and would never extend enough help to allow America to break from its grip. He was undiplomatic enough to express those sentiments in a series of letters to the French foreign minister the count de Vergennes, who found the correspondence so exasperating that he refused to deal further with Adams.

Moreover, he asked Franklin to send the letters home to the Congress so that it might decide whether Adams was the man for such an important job.

Meanwhile, Franklin pursued his hope of a substantial loan. In desperation he asked Vergennes for 25 million French livres. In the end he got a promise of 6 million, enough at least to keep America in the fight. But at 75, Franklin was beginning to find his responsibilities in France exhausting. Two years earlier his enemies in America, led by the tireless Arthur Lee and his brother Richard, had succeeded in sowing doubts about Franklin among some members of the Congress. They accused him of excessive attachment to France and its interests, of "weaving little plots." In a campaign that especially pained Franklin, they demanded that his grandson Temple be recalled from his job as secretary to Franklin, not only on grounds of nepotism, but also because he was suspect as the son of a loyalist governor. Franklin wrote in anger to his son-in-law, Richard Bache: "It is enough I have lost my son; would they add my grandson!"

VICTORY ON LAND *As George Washington looks on, Gen. Benjamin Lincoln accepts the surrender of the British at Yorktown.*

LA BELLE VIE IN FRANCE

In France, Franklin became a man in full, an ambassador pitch-perfect in temperament and talent to conduct the urgent business of his new country. Soon enough he had insinuated himself into the national psyche, becoming a beloved national treasure, while learning the language, charming nobles and intellectuals, having a wonderful time—and getting exactly what he wanted for the new United States. Given how agreeable the life there was for him, is it any surprise that he found reasons to remain in France for several years after his main business as a diplomat was completed?

THE CRAZE FOR MESMER

In 1784 an unorthodox German healer, Friedrich Anton Mesmer, left, captivated Paris with theories of "animal magnetism." He claimed to cure illnesses by stroking patients with magnets in group sessions that also involved hypnotism—"mesmerism." Asked to join a royal commission to investigate Mesmer's claims, Franklin, above, allowed himself to be subjected to Mesmer's procedure. The commission concluded that Mesmer was a fraud.

UP, UP AND AWAY

In 1783 Franklin—with much of France—was fascinated by ballooning. That year the Montgolfier brothers, Etienne and Joseph, launched the first hot-air balloons. In September, Franklin was part of a crowd, at left, that watched the launch of the first balloon lifted by hydrogen. By the end of the year he had helped finance the first manned flight of a hydrogen balloon. When someone asked him what good was all this ballooning business, he offered a witty reply: "What good is a newborn baby?"

107

BON VIVANT

The estate where he lived in the village of Passy, with its broad gardens, above, was a plush haven for Franklin. At right, his own sketch of a corner of the garden. At top, a drawing by his grandson Benny of the chateau. Upon witnessing Franklin's idyllic life and the many people who came to pay him court, John Adams was taken aback: "It was late when he breakfasted, and as soon as breakfast was over, a crowd of carriages came … He was invited to dine every day … He came home at all hours from nine to twelve o'clock at night."

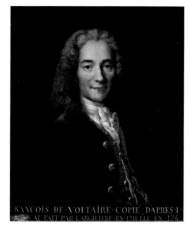

Franklin presentant a Voltaire son petit fils de lui demandant sa Benediction
celui ci l'ayant la main sur la tête, l'Enfant, en di God and Liberty!
Dieu et la liberté!

MUTUAL ADMIRATION

After two decades in exile, Voltaire returned to Paris in 1778 to spend the last three months of his life. Two of the 300 people who came to see him there were Franklin and his grandson Benny. As seen at left in a contemporary drawing, Voltaire offered Benny his blessing, placing his hand on the boy's head and saying, in English, "God and Liberty."

SECOND ESTATE

The French royal family, at left, gathers around the dauphin. French royals and aristocrats were intrigued by Franklin—his bald head and Quaker clothing, disarming intellect and charm. Ladies were so taken with his soft fur cap that they copied it into a hairstyle known as the coiffure à la Franklin. *Despite his credentials as a man of the people, Franklin was no less charmed by the French noblemen—and the equally delightful noblewomen—and spent many happy hours in their company.*

In April 1779, Congress went so far as to debate whether to recall Franklin and the other commissioners. Thanks largely to French insistence that Franklin keep his job, he did, but the experience left bruised feelings. In March 1781, after the new French loan was secured, Franklin offered to resign. In a letter to Congress he claimed that he had enjoyed "honor sufficient to satisfy any reasonable ambition, and I have no other left but that of repose, which I hope Congress will grant me."

Repose would have to wait. Instead Congress decided to add to Franklin's duties in France. Adams would no longer be the sole future negotiator with Britain. That would now be the job of a five-member commission that would include Adams, Thomas Jefferson, John Jay of New York, and Henry Laurens of South Carolina—and Franklin. Even better, in response to a request from French Foreign Minister Vergennes, who had lobbied for Franklin's inclusion on the commission, the Congress directed the commissioners to do nothing in any negotiations without French knowledge and approval. Better still, Temple was appointed secretary to the new commission.

In autumn came the best news. All summer Gen. Cornwallis, commander of the British forces in the South, had been conducting campaigns in Virginia in the hope of luring George Washington to

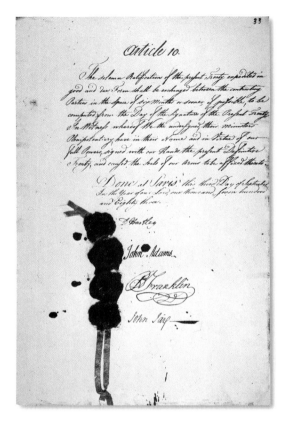

HALF THE PEACEMAKERS
Because the British negotiators did not pose, the American painter Benjamin West could not finish his portrait, at left, of the men who concluded the Treaty of Paris. But he managed to show the American side. From left, John Jay, John Adams, Franklin, Henry Laurens, and their secretary, Franklin's grandson Temple. Above, the treaty.

engage in a major battle there. Washington did not begin to take the bait until he got word that a French fleet of 29 ships carrying 3,000 troops was on its way from the West Indies. When the battle finally began in October, at Yorktown, 9,000 French soldiers marched alongside 11,000 Americans, while the French ships clogged the mouth of the Chesapeake and prevented a British naval rescue of the trapped Cornwallis. For days American and French cannon fire decimated the British ranks. On Oct. 17, Cornwallis surrendered. The war was over. The Americans—the inexperienced, underfunded, ever-beleaguered Americans!—had won.

Now came the hard part.

NEGOTIATING THE PEACE Franklin knew there were people who doubted his qualifications to negotiate a settlement with Britain, and not just because of his presumed attachment to France. He was, after all, the man who had repeatedly expressed the view he put succinctly in a letter to his friend Jonathan Shipley. "There has never been, nor ever will be, any such thing as a good war, or a bad peace." Was this the man to make a shrewd peace?

In any event, talks could not get under way until March 1782, when a new British government headed by Lord Rockingham was in place. At the time, Franklin was the only one of the five American negotiators in Paris, where the talks would take place. Thomas Jefferson had declined the job. Henry Laurens had been captured at sea by the British and imprisoned. Meanwhile Adams and Jay were on the Continent. For a few months Franklin had the field to himself.

From the first there was a built-in complication in the talks. The Americans had been directed by the Congress to coordinate their actions with the French. But the British wanted separate talks and a separate peace with America. The first of their negotiators arrived in April. Richard Oswald, a retired London merchant who had lived for a time in America, was effectively the agent of Britain's colonial secretary Lord Shelburne in Shelburne's rivalry with the foreign secretary, Charles Fox. Hardly had he arrived in Paris than Oswald, genial but persistent, began pressing a wary Franklin for one-on-one talks. Why should peace between America and Britain be detained, Oswald wanted to know, by issues of more concern to France and Spain? (Whether Spain or Britain should have ownership of Gibraltar, for instance.) Franklin had his own preoccupations. Shouldn't Britain pay reparations to its former colonies for war damage? Franklin even had in mind what a fair compensation might be—Canada. Oswald promised to convey the idea to Lord Shelburne. Franklin later wrote, "We parted exceeding good friends." In the final peace, however, Canada would not change hands.

Within a month there was a second, less agreeable British envoy, the 27-year-old Thomas Grenville, son of the George Grenville who was behind the Stamp Act. He came as the representative of

Lord Shelburne's rival, Fox. But it was Grenville's mission as well to encourage separate talks between Britain and America. What followed was six months of complex gamesmanship in which Franklin maneuvered among the two British envoys, not always keeping Vergennes in the loop, as he became convinced that it was in America's interest to deal separately with Britain. By July, Shelburne had become Prime Minister, Fox had resigned, and Grenville had been recalled. Franklin seized the opportunity to make a specific peace proposal to Oswald—without informing Vergennes. The complexities multiplied when Jay, who was much more suspicious of the French, returned to Paris and became lead American negotiator while Franklin was ill with gout and kidney stones.

In the end America and Britain would indeed conclude a separate peace, one they signed on Nov. 30, though by agreement it would not go into effect until there was also a treaty between France and England. That came nine months later. It fell to Franklin to write a very diplomatic letter to Vergennes explaining why the Americans had acted on their own, while assuring him of America's continuing friendship. He also managed to get from the aggrieved French yet another loan for America.

LAST YEARS IN PASSY With his final mission accomplished, Franklin could relax again at Passy. He would remain in France for another two and a half years, enjoying the sweetness of life and the affection of the French people. It was time to summon his grandson Benny Bache back from the school in Switzerland where he had been miserably stashed for three years. Meanwhile grandson Temple found time to father an illegitimate son by a married woman, thus establishing the family's third generation of illegitimate boys. But the child would shortly die of smallpox.

The end of the war also offered what might have been an opportunity for Franklin to reconcile with his son William, who had resettled in England and written to his father from there. Franklin agreed to allow Temple to visit William in London in the fall of 1784—but also coolly put William on notice not to introduce Temple "to company that it may be improper for him to be seen with."

"Life is a kind of Chess, in which we have often Points to gain, and Competitors or Adversaries to contend with … The game is so full of events … that one is encouraged to continue the contest to the last, in hopes of Victory from our own skill."
—BENJAMIN FRANKLIN, *The Morals of Chess, June 1779*

THE GREAT GAME
Franklin was an avid chess player. A few years before negotiating the peace with England he wrote an essay on the game full of hints about his diplomacy. This chess set was passed down in his family and said to be his.

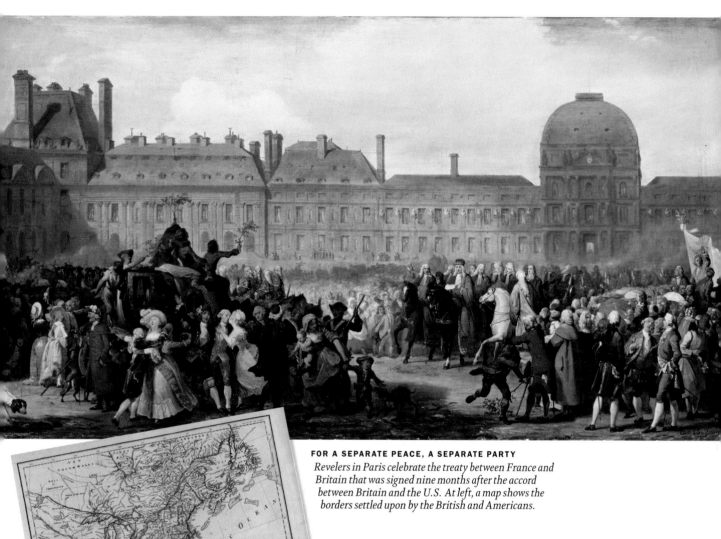

FOR A SEPARATE PEACE, A SEPARATE PARTY
Revelers in Paris celebrate the treaty between France and Britain that was signed nine months after the accord between Britain and the U.S. At left, a map shows the borders settled upon by the British and Americans.

By the next year Franklin knew it was time to leave. In May he stepped down as American minister to France. He would be replaced by Thomas Jefferson, who had arrived in Paris the preceding summer. His French friends pleaded with him to stay among them, especially Mesdames Brillon and Helvétius. But though he dreaded the prospect of yet another ocean voyage, Franklin wanted to spend his last years in the America he had done so much to foster and defend. On July 12, Marie Antoinette sent her royal litter to take him from Passy to Le Havre. There a channel boat took him to Southampton, where he could find a British vessel to take him home.

But first there would be a meeting in Southampton with William. A meeting, but not a reconciliation. Instead Franklin and his son would have a blunt discussion about money and property. Franklin required William to repay him for debts accumulated over the years, to sell to Temple his farm in New Jersey, and to hand over his land claims in New York. A few days later Franklin and his grandsons boarded ship for home. He would never see William again. ■

DRAMAS OF
THE FINAL ACT

As usual Franklin made the most of his time during the transatlantic voyage. On previous trips he had studied the calming effect of oil on turbulent water and the motions of the Gulf Stream. This time he produced a notebook full of observations, theories, and drawings related to a whole multitude of questions from ship design to the problem of household chimney smoke. His body was failing, his kidney stone was a perennial trial, but his mind was as sharp as ever.

Franklin arrived in Philadelphia much as he'd left Passy—as a hero. He was met at the pier by the gratifying noise of crowds, cannons, and bells, all celebrating his return. It wasn't long before he was chosen head of Pennsylvania's Executive Council, a body he had created when he presided over the writing of the state's constitution in 1776. Later the Philadelphia artist Charles Willson Peale came by to paint a portrait of Franklin wearing the bifocals he had invented in France. Peale used the painting as the basis for a series of mezzotint prints that were soon to be seen all around the city.

Having settled at last into the house on Market Street he had scarcely ever lived in, Franklin was surrounded by family—his daughter, Sally, her husband, Richard Bache, and their six children. It was a brood sizable enough to require Franklin to enlarge the house by almost a third, with a spacious new library that took up the entire second floor, a room

BUSTLING PHILLY
Much was new in the city Franklin returned to. But he would have recognized the steeple of Christ Church, where he worshiped, and Town Hall, at left.

big enough to hold his more than 4,200 books. Still very much the inventor, he designed a mechanical arm that let him take down and return books from high shelves. And for his comfort he produced a chair with an overhead fan that could be operated by a foot pedal.

He also tore down three old houses that were at the front of his lot on Market Street and replaced them with two new ones. One would be occupied by the print shop of his grandson Benny, who was to enter his grandfather's trade after he finished his studies at the academy—now called the University of the State of Pennsylvania—his grandfather had founded. Meanwhile, Temple was busying himself, none too effectively, on the New Jersey farm that Franklin had obliged his son William to sell.

Franklin's days of roaming the world, or even just North America, were over. His kidney stone made it impossible for him to travel by horseback or carriage. But he had looked forward anyway to a quiet life in Philadelphia and for a time he found it. Many of the friends from his Junto had passed on, but enough of the old-timers had survived that he could still hold meetings of his American Philosophical Society and even his volunteer fire company. He could lose himself for hours in the card game called cribbage. "I have public business enough to preserve me from ennui," he reported to a friend, "and private amusement besides in conversation, books, my garden, and cribbage." As he approached 80, it may have been reasonable for him to suppose that the major episodes of his long life were all behind him. But remarkably there was one more great event in which he would play a part—the framing of the United States Constitution.

THE CONSTITUTIONAL CONVENTION By 1786 the flaws in the Articles of Confederation that governed the new nation were apparent. The weak central authority that the Articles created was insufficient to essential tasks like settling disputes among the states or compelling them to pay the costs of the national government. Then, in the summer of that year, a rebellion broke out in Massachusetts that put all its failings in high relief. Farmers hard-pressed by debt wanted the state legislature to issue paper money to stimulate the economy. They also wanted to stop the courts from confiscating debtor property. When neither happened, they rose up with guns in their hands. Under the leadership of a Revolutionary War veteran named Daniel Shays, more than 1,000 armed insurgents forced courts in the central and Western parts of the state to shut down.

Though Shays' Rebellion was eventually suppressed—mostly by a hastily assembled militia financed privately by nervous businessmen in Boston—the tardy response of government laid bare its inability even to keep the peace. In September representatives from five states meeting in Annapolis, Md., issued a call for a larger convocation in Philadelphia the following May. Its purpose was supposed to be to revise the Articles. In fact it would produce an entirely and radically new document.

Naturally, Franklin was chosen to be part of Pennsylvania's delegation to what we now call the Constitutional Convention. The garden of his home on Market Street, not far from the Pennsylvania statehouse where the Convention was held, would also become a place delegates could repair to for refreshments and conversation under the shade of Franklin's mulberry tree. It would be a respite

"If it does not do good it will do harm, as it will show that we have not the wisdom enough among us to govern ourselves."
— BENJAMIN FRANKLIN, *in a letter to Thomas Jefferson on the Constitutional Convention*

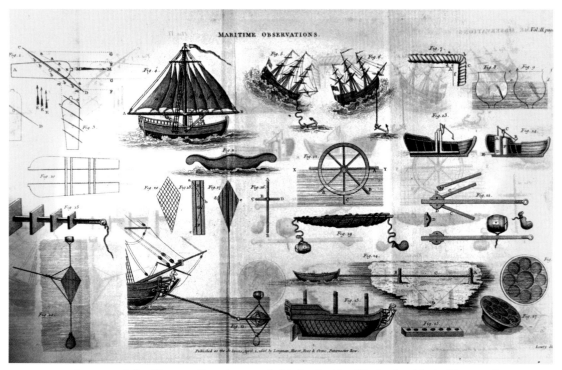

SHIP SHAPES *An engraved plate illustrates ideas about nautical design that Franklin developed during his voyage home.*

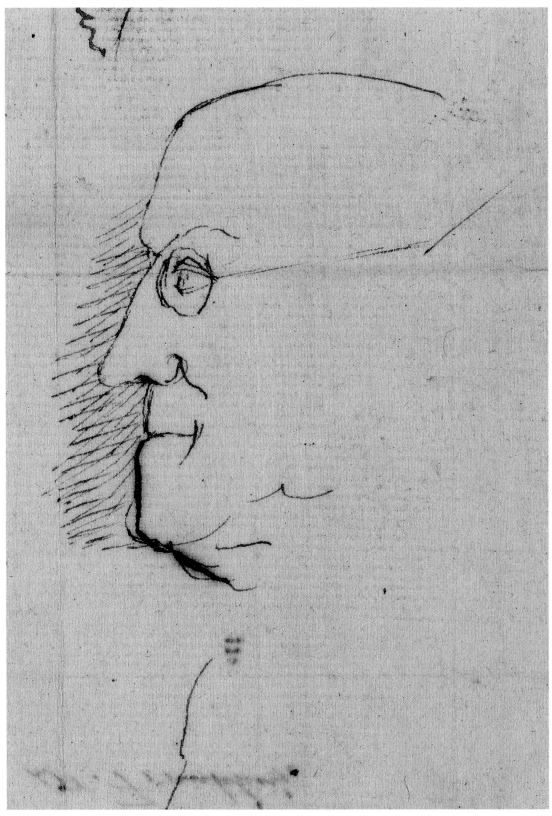

LATE HEADLINE *This profile of Franklin in old age is believed to have been drawn by his grandson Benny Bache.*

> "The longer I live, the more convincing proofs I see of this truth—that God governs in the affairs of men."
>
> — BENJAMIN FRANKLIN, *addressing the Convention*

NOT EVERYBODY LOVED HIM
Because Franklin's almanacs and journalism adapted maxims by other writers, a British cartoon attacks him as a plagiarist making money off their words.

from the stifling hall where the windows were kept shut so that the delegates could pursue their controversial work in secret. There were people all around the colonies who might have demanded a halt to the proceedings if they knew how far the Convention would go in laying down a blueprint for a more powerful central government.

Because of the difficulties he had with walking, Franklin is reported to have arrived at the Convention on its first day in grand style, borne in a sedan chair carried by four prisoners from the local jail. As he had been at the Continental Congress, he would be again by far the oldest man attending this assembly, and also just as before one of the quietest. When he did have something to say, to spare himself the discomfort of being on his feet, he often wrote out his remarks for others to deliver on his behalf.

In any event most of the ideas Franklin would recommend to the meeting would be rejected. He tried in vain to promote the idea of a one-chamber legislature of the kind he had designed for Pennsylvania—and which even Pennsylvania would discard when it revised its state constitution. He proposed, to no effect, that the new national government should have an executive council instead of an individual president. He even put forward that members of the council should serve without pay. Franklin's views on that matter had been shaped in England, where he had seen the corrupt pursuit of office for the income that came with it. "In all cases of public service," he said, "the less the profit the greater the honor." Did he see the risk that his plan might limit government service almost entirely to men rich enough to have no need of a salary? No matter—his motion was quietly tabled and buried.

Yet Franklin would still provide one indispensable service to the Convention by promoting compromise on one of its most difficult issues. Should representatives to the legislature be chosen by population, with large states having more representatives than small ones? Or should each state have an equal number, as they did under the Articles? It was a debate that threatened to paralyze the delegates. As a first step, Franklin wrote out a lengthy address, read aloud on June 11 by one of his

UNCOMMON CURRENCY
The first coin authorized by Congress was a one cent bearing a design believed to have been suggested by Franklin. On its face, at left, was a sundial and the Latin word "Fugio"— I fly. On the reverse, far left, the motto "We are one" was surrounded by the words "United States" and set within a circle of 13 linked rings, representing the 13 original states.

stand-ins, that pleaded for flexibility. "Declarations of a fixed opinion," he told the other delegates, "and of determined resolution never to change it, neither enlighten nor convince us."

In the same entreaty he put forward a few ideas for compromise, most of them unlikely. (One example: Large states might pass land to smaller ones to make them all more nearly equal in size.) But later that day a more workable idea was put forward by Roger Sherman of Connecticut. Why not a House of Representatives proportionally chosen by population and a Senate where every state had equal representation? It was a proposal that seemed to offer something to everyone, yet initially it was voted down, and in the days that followed, debate on the question grew increasingly testy.

One more time Franklin stepped forward in his role as conciliator. On June 30, after making another plea for cooperation, he put the Connecticut Compromise into specific terms that he presented to the Convention for a vote. The legislature would consist of a lower house that would be elected proportionally and a Senate in which each state would send an equal number of representatives. Due partly to Franklin's prestige within the convention, on July 16 the proposal was adopted, opening the way at last to the completion of the Convention's work. It would be the old man's last great service to his nation.

WE THE PEOPLE
Franklin's printed copy of the Constitution, with his handwritten annotations. Confronted by a woman who asked what type of government the Convention had produced, he replied: "A republic, madam, if you can keep it."

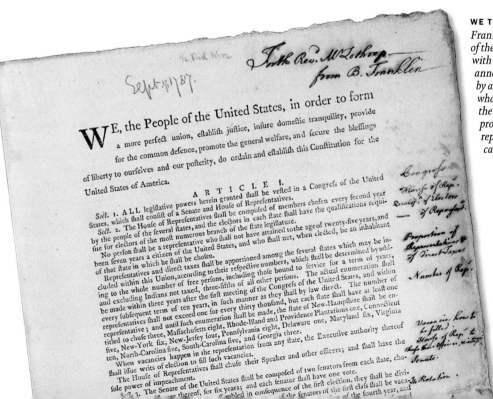

Slavery's Foe, At Last

BY GARY B. NASH

ABOLITION! *Franklin owned this widely circulated medallion by the English potter Josiah Wedgwood.*

Over a long life, Benjamin Franklin remained engaged with slavery as a buyer, seller, and master of slaves—but finally as an abolitionist.

Franklin and his wife, Deborah, purchased slaves—Peter and Jemima—for the first time in the late 1740s, but he was uneasy about keeping them in the succession of small rented houses where the Franklins lived. Franklin believed that owning slaves diminished the master's work ethic and ruined the white children in the families that owned them because they are "educated in idleness." Yet, while rearing son William, the Franklins bought more slaves, named Othello, King, and George. The last two were in tow when Franklin and William left for England in 1757.

To Franklin's dismay, King fled when his master was visiting outside London. He was later found in Suffolk in the service of a lady who had taught him to read and write and to play the violin and French horn. Franklin, who agreed to sell King to the woman, may have appreciated the slave's newfound skills because, at the time, Franklin was revising his opinion about Africans' capabilities. A few years later, after visiting an Anglican school for blacks in Philadelphia, he concluded, "Their apprehension seems as quick, their memory as strong, and their docility in every respect equal to that of white children."

By 1772 Franklin was openly questioning the morality of slavery. In an unsigned letter to the *London Chronicle*, he asked readers whether it was absolutely necessary to sweeten their tea with slave-produced sugar. Could such a "petty pleasure…compensate for so much misery produced among our fellow creatures, and such a constant butchery of the human species by this pestilential detestable traffic in the bodies and souls of men?"

Despite such pronouncements, Franklin and his wife held on to their slaves. But by his 81st birthday, Franklin was speaking openly against slavery. Accepting the ceremonial presidency of the Pennsylvania Abolition Society, he signed a public exhortation that declared "the Creator of the world" made "of one flesh, all the children of men." Still, the surviving records from the Constitutional Convention give no indication that Franklin raised the issue there.

Just before he died, Franklin had his last words on the subject in a biting parody. He composed a speech allegedly by one Sidi Mehemet Ibrahim, an Algerian prince, defending the practice of enslaving Christians. "If we forbear to make Slaves of [the Christians]," asked the prince, "who in this hot climate are to cultivate our lands? Who are to perform the common Labours of our City, and in our Families?" Yet Franklin's rhetoric outpaced his actions. He had long ago revised his will to free Peter and Jemima at his death, but neither slave outlived him. ■

Gary B. Nash is the author of Forging Freedom: The Formation of Philadelphia's Black Community, 1720-1840.

LAST RESTING PLACES *The Philadelphia gravesite of Franklin and wife Deborah. Beside them are their daughter and son-in-law.*

THE FINAL DAYS For all his maladies, Franklin would live on for nearly three more years, time enough to accept one more yearlong term as "president" of Pennsylvania and to return to work on his *Autobiography*, which he would take up to the time he arrived in England, but never complete. He continued to live in the house on Market Street, where Polly Stevenson, the now widowed daughter of his London landlady, had come to join the Franklin-Bache household with her son.

There would even be one last crusade. For most of his adult life Franklin owned slaves as household servants. But in his later years he became convinced that slavery was an evil that must be eradicated. In 1787 he accepted the presidency of the Pennsylvania Society for Promoting the Abolition of Slavery and published a plan detailing ways that freed blacks could be absorbed into society. In his capacity as president of the Society he also presented Congress with a petition calling upon it to grant "liberty to those unhappy men who alone in this land of freedom are degraded into perpetual bondage."

That was in February. In April, Franklin dictated his last letter, to Thomas Jefferson. Soon after, he developed what appears to have been a lung infection. Fever and pain set in. For 10 days he was confined to his bed, rising just once so it could be made up and he might, as he said, "die in a decent manner." Finally an abscess in his lung burst. On the night of April 17, 1790, with his grandsons Temple and Benny at his bedside, the 84-year-old Franklin slipped away.

Among the provisions of his will—in which he pointedly left almost nothing to his son William—Franklin provided a fund to make loans to young tradesmen in Boston and Philadelphia, with a stipulation that the money and its accrued growth should pass to the public treasury in 200 years. By the 1990s, after two centuries of investment and increase, that same fund was worth millions of dollars in both cities, where it was released to be distributed across a variety of projects. It was Franklin's final—and typically prudent and industrious—gift to the nation he had done so much to create. ∎

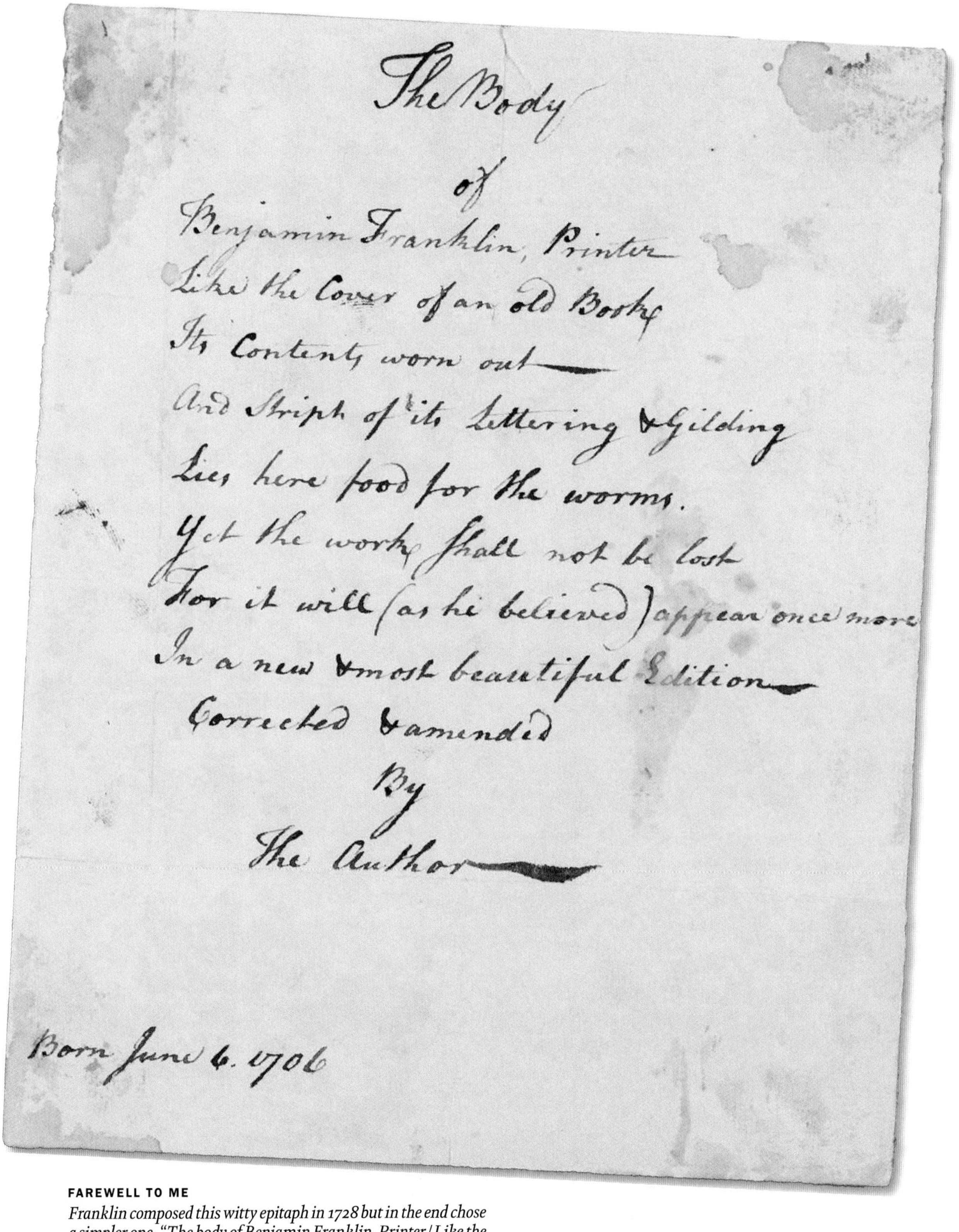

The Body

of

Benjamin Franklin, Printer
Like the Cover of an old Book,
Its Contents worn out—
And Stript of its Lettering & Gilding
Lies here food for the worms.
Yet the work shall not be lost
For it will (as he believed) appear once more
In a new & most beautiful Edition
Corrected & amended

By

The Author—

Born June 6. 1706

FAREWELL TO ME
Franklin composed this witty epitaph in 1728 but in the end chose a simpler one. "The body of Benjamin Franklin, Printer / Like the cover of an old book / Its contents worn out / And stript of its lettering and gilding / Lies here, food for the worms / Yet the work shall not be lost / For it will (as he believed) appear once more / In a new and more beautiful edition / Corrected and amended By the Author."

MR. FRANKLIN'S NEIGHBORHOODS *Sites in Philadelphia associated with Franklin include, from left, Independence Hall, Franklin National Memorial, Robert Venturi's representation of his house, and Franklin Court on Market Street.*

In the City That Ben Loved

By Heather Won Tesoriero

Ben Franklin liked to think of himself first and foremost as a printer, and his imprint on his adopted hometown of Philadelphia hasn't faded with the years. If you're seeking to follow in his footsteps there, you can hear the music of the colonial glass armonica he invented, visit places where he lived, and even dine at his favorite tavern for a bite of colonial turkey potpie.

A good place to start your visit is the **Benjamin Franklin National Memorial,** which is positioned at the entrance to the **Franklin Institute** (fi.edu), the city's expansive science museum. The cavernous inner dome houses a big Ben statue built to the same scale as the Lincoln Memorial. The museum's ode to Ben, displaying some of his many inventions, is a permanent exhibit called "Franklin...He's Electric." You can see an electrostatic machine, a clever long-reach device, and a pair of swim fins (yes, he invented those too).

A 10-minute cab ride across town will land you in the **Old City,** where Franklin sites are clustered within walking distance. Most of them are run by the National Park Service, which gives excellent free daily tours.

Right across the street from **Independence Hall** in the Old City is the **American Philosophical Society** (amphilsoc.org), founded by Franklin in 1743. (At the time, natural—as opposed to moral—philosophy referred to science.)

Accessible from Market and Chestnut streets is **Franklin Court,** site of Franklin's home. Completed in 1766, the house was an object of great pride for Franklin, particularly the third-floor music room. Franklin chose this site for its strategic and symbolic

value; determined to honor his leather-apron roots, he built the courtyard on a spot that lay squarely between posh and working-class neighborhoods. After he died, Franklin's grandchildren razed the place, thinking the property was worth more than the home. In 1976 architect Robert Venturi's ghost structure—a beam outline (to scale) of the home—was erected.

An operating post office and the **Franklin Court Printing Office** are situated next to the Market Street entrance to Franklin Court. The post office is the only one in the U.S. that does not fly a flag, because when Franklin was appointed the first American postmaster general, in 1775, the nation had not yet come into being.

Head down Market Street toward the Delaware River, and tucked back on Second and Church streets is **Christ Church,** which Franklin attended. Parishioners rented their pews in those days, and Franklin chose Pew 70, a little more than halfway back from the altar. Not wanting to have a showy front-row seat, he maintained that he could hear fine from his pew. Plus, having a pew in the middle meant he could arrive late and leave early, and his dozing was less visible.

Walk north on Second Street, and you will hit **Elfreth's Alley,** believed to be the oldest residential street in the U.S. You may notice tiny mirrors jutting from the top floors. Called busybodies, these contraptions, which enable people to see who is coming down the street, were brought back from Holland by Franklin. Also look out for black iron plaques that depict four fists locked in the firefighter's carry. These plaques indicated that a house was insured against fire, insurance being one of Franklin's imports from London.

Franklin, who enjoyed many of his meals at **City Tavern,** would be pleased to see that the replica of the original, which burned in 1834, honors its predecessor's layout and even the apparel of the 18th-century serving staff. The authentic recipes for such fare as apple-wood-smoked pork chops give diners a taste of the past.

Picture Credits

COVER
Benjamin Franklin by Joseph Siffred Duplessis, c. 1785, Gift of the Morris and Gwendolyn Cafritz Foundation, National Portrait Gallery, Smithsonian Institution—Art Resource, N.Y. (detail)

BACK COVER
Granger Collection (2)

TITLE
1 Silk suit made for Franklin during his years at Passy by La Hure (attributed), Massachusetts Historical Society

MASTHEAD
3 SSPL—Getty Images

CONTENTS
4–5 (clockwise from top left) Benjamin Franklin c. 1746 by Robert Feke (attributed), Harvard Art Museum, Fogg Art Museum, Harvard University Portrait Collection, Bequest of Dr. John Collins Warren, 1856, photo by Katya Kallsen—President and Fellows of Harvard College; Pen and Brown Ink on Paper Drawing of Benjamin Franklin by Jacques-Louis David (attributed), Gift of David P. Willis—Rosenbach Museum & Library, Philadelphia; Benjamin Franklin by Mason Chamberlain, 1762, Gift of Mr. and Mrs. Wharton Sinkler, 1956, Philadelphia Museum of Art—Art Resource, N.Y.; Benjamin Franklin by Charles Willson Peale, 1789, Atwater Kent Museum of Philadelphia, The Historical Society of Pennsylvania Collection—The Bridgeman Art Library International; Bust of Benjamin Franklin by Jean Antoine Houdon, 1779, Philadelphia Museum of Art, Photo by Graydin Wood—Courtesy of the Benjamin Franklin Tercentenary; Benjamin Franklin by Joseph Siffred Duplessis, c. 1778, Harvard Art Museum, Fogg Art Museum, Bequest of Grenville L. Winthrop, 1942.235—Harvard College

INTRODUCTION
7 Benjamin Franklin Drawing Electricity from the Sky by Benjamin West, c. 1816, Gift of Mr. and Mrs. Wharton Sinkler, Philadelphia Museum of Art—Art Resource, N.Y.

TIMELINE
8–9 (top to bottom, left to right) Bettmann Corbis; Granger Collection (2) Deborah Read Franklin by Benjamin Wilson (attributed), c. 1759—American Philosophical Society; Rosenbach Museum & Library, Philadelphia—Courtesy of The Benjamin Franklin Tercentenary; Granger Collection; Henry Steeper and John Dawkins: A South East Prospect of the Pennsylvania Hospital with the Elevation of the Intended Plan, 1755—The Library Company of Philadelphia; Granger Collection; Library of Congress; Glass Armonica (English), Charles James (designed by Benjamin Franklin), The Frankliniana Collection, The Franklin Institute, Inc., Photo by Peter Harholdt—Courtesy of The Benjamin Franklin Tercentenary; Atwater Kent Museum of Philadelphia—The Bridgeman Art Library International; Courtesy of the Massachusetts Historical Society; Granger Collection; no credit; American Commissioners of the Preliminary Peace Negotiations with Great Britain, 1783-1785 by Benjamin West (attributed)—Winterthur Museum, Garden and Library; SSPL—The Image Works; Benjamin Franklin by Jacques Thouron, Photo by Jean

Popovitch, Louvre, Réunion des Musées Nationaux—Art Resource, N.Y.

CHAPTER 1
11 (top) Peter Frank Chapman; Granger Collection (2) **12** (right) King Charles II by Godfrey Kneller, Powis Castle, Wales, Great Britain, Photo by Clare Bates, National Trust Photo Library—Art Resource, N.Y.; (left) Granger Collection (2) **13** (top) Granger Collection; Abiah Folger Franklin by Gerrit Duyckinck (attributed), 1707, Photo Courtesy of Melissa Williams Fine Art **14** Harvard University by William Burgis c. 1725-26—Granger Collection; **15** Map of Boston by John Bonner, 1722—Granger Collection **16** Granger Collection **17** American Philosophical Society **18** (left to right) Frontispiece and Title Page from John Bunyan's The Pilgrim's Progress 1684—Corbis; Frontispiece of Plutarch's Lives 1656—Private Collection—The Bridgeman Art Library International; no credit **19** Granger Collection **20** (top) Lake County Museum—Corbis; From the Historical and Interpretive Collections of the Franklin Institute, Inc., Philadelphia, Pa. (4) **21** (top to bottom) Courtesy of The Massachusetts Historical Society; Philadelphia History Museum at the Atwater Kent, The Historical Society of Pennsylvania Collection—Photo by Peter Harholdt; Granger Collection **22** (clockwise from top left) Library of Congress (3); Beinecke Rare Book and Manuscript Library, Library of Congress; Beinecke Rare Book and Manuscript Library, Yale University **23** Lake County Museum—Corbis **24** Courtesy of the Massachusetts Historical Society **25** (left) Granger Collection; (right) Edward Jenner Performing the First Vaccination Against Smallpox in 1796 (detail), 1879, Melingue, Gaston, Academie Nationale de Medecine, Paris, France, Archives Charmet—The Bridgeman Art Library International; (bottom) Granger Collection

CHAPTER 2
26 East Prospective View of Philadelphia, 1778 lithograph from 1754 drawing by George Heap, Photo by Michael Sheldon—Art Resource, N.Y. **28** Kean Collection—Getty Images **29** Granger Collection **30** (top) A Rake's Progress III: The Rake at the Rose-Tavern by William Hogarth, 1734, Courtesy of the Trustees of Sir John Soane's Museum, London—The Bridgeman Art Library International; Library of Congress **31** Map of London 1724, Historical Picture Archive—Corbis **32** Bettmann Corbis **33** American Philosophical Society **34** Granger Collection **35** (left to right) Herbert Orth—Time Life Pictures; Walter J. and Leonore Annenberg Rare Book and Manuscript Library, U. of Pennsylvania, Philadelphia; Embroidered Silk Sash, Collection of the Grand Lodge of Free and Accepted Masons of Pennsylvania (Philadelphia)—Photo by Peter Harholdt **36** (left) Deborah Read Franklin by Benjamin Wilson (attributed), c. 1759—American Philosophical Society; "Franky" Franklin by Samuel Johnson (attributed), Private Collection—Photo by Peter Harholdt **37** Granger Collection **38** Rosenbach Museum & Library, Philadelphia—Courtesy of the Benjamin Franklin Tercentenary **39** Granger Collection **40** (clockwise from upper left) Granger Collection; American Philosophical Society; The Library Company of Philadelphia (Philadelphia, Pa.) **41** (top) Getty Images; Andreas Feininger—Time Life Pictures **42** (left) The Battery, detail of The East Prospect of the City of Philadelphia by George Heap, in the London Magazine (London, October, 1761)—The Library Company of Philadelphia; Lottery ticket, Third Class by B. Franklin and D. Hall, 1748, Historical Society of Pennsylvania **43** Benjamin Franklin c. 1746 by Robert Feke (attributed), Harvard Art Museum, Fogg Art

Museum, Harvard University Portrait Collection, Bequest of Dr. John Collins Warren, 1856, Photo by Katya Kallsen—Harvard University **44** Granger Collection **45** Granger Collection

CHAPTER 3
47 A South East Prospect of the Pennsylvania Hospital with the Elevation of the intended plan by Henry Steeper and John Dawkins, 1755—The Library Company of Philadelphia **48** (top) Bettmann Corbis; Granger Collection **49** Map of Philadelphia and Parts Adjacent, 1753, Nicholas Scull and George Heap—The Library Company of Philadelphia **50** Currier & Ives lithograph—Granger Collection **52** (clockwise from top) Musee de la Cooperation Franco-Americaine, Blerancourt, France, Photo by Erich Lessing—Art Resource, N.Y.; Corbis; The Library Company of Philadelphia **53** (clockwise from top left) Frankliniana Collection, The Franklin Institute, Inc., Benjamin Franklin Tercentenary—Photo by Peter Harholdt; SSPL—The Image Works; American Philosophical Society, Benjamin Franklin Tercentenary—Photo by Peter Harholdt **54** (top) Corbis; Glass Armonica, Charles James (designed by Benjamin Franklin), The Frankliniana Collection, The Franklin Institute, Inc.— Photo by Peter Harholdt **55** (clockwise from top left) Library of Congress; American Philosophical Society—Photo by Peter Harholdt; Ted Thai—Time Life Pictures; Hulton Archive—Getty Images **56** Benjamin Franklin by Mason Chamberlain, 1762, Gift of Mr. and Mrs. Wharton Sinkler, 1956, Philadelphia Museum of Art—Art Resource, N.Y. **57** Library of Congress (2) **58** Atwater Kent Museum of Philadelphia—The Bridgeman Art Library International **59** Courtesy of The Newberry Library **60** Lake County Museum—Corbis **61** (top) The Wounding of General Braddock by Robert Griffing—Courtesy of Paramount Press Inc. and The Westmoreland Museum of Fine Art; Granger Collection

CHAPTER 4
63 Benjamin Franklin by David Martin, 1767—The White House Historical Association (White House Collection) **64** Thomas Penn by M.J. Naylor after Joseph Highmore—Philadelphia History Museum at the Atwater Kent **65** Sketch of Benjamin Franklin and a Lady by Charles Willson Peale, c.1767—American Philosophical Society; Granger Collection **66** Collection of the Grand Lodge of Free and Accepted Masons of Pennsylvania (Philadelphia, Pa.)—Photo by Peter Harholdt **67** Northumberland House by Giovanni Antonio Canal Canaletto, 1752, Private Collection—The Bridgeman Art Library International **68** William Franklin by Mather Brown (attributed) ca. 1760s—Private Collection **69** Granger Collection (2) **70** (top) The Library Company of Philadelphia; Mansell Collection—Time Life Pictures **71** (clockwise from left) Library of Congress; George Grenville lithograph by Richard Houston, Leeds Museums and Galleries, City Art Gallery, U.K.—The Bridgeman Art Library International; Courtesy of The Massachusetts Historical Society **72** (top) Granger Collection; Mrs. Richard Bache (Sarah Franklin) by John Hoppner, 1793, Catherine Lorillard Wolfe Collection, Wolfe Fund, 1901, The Metropolitan Museum of Art, N.Y.—Art Resource, N.Y. **73** Granger Collection **75** (left) Madame Helvetius (Anne-Catherine de Ligniville d'Autricourt) by Louis-Michel Van Loo—La Caisse Nationale des Monuments Historiques et des Sites; Private Collection—Photo Courtesy of Conservation Center for Art & Historical Artifacts **76** (clockwise from top left) David Hume by Allan Ramsey, 1766, Scottish National Portrait Gallery, Edinburgh, Scotland—The Bridgeman Art Library International; William Strahan by Sir Joshua Reynolds—National Portrait Gallery, London; James Boswell by George Willison, 1765, Scottish

National Portrait Gallery, Edinburgh, Scotland—The Bridgeman Art Library International **77** The Coffee House Orator by Edgar Bundy, Rochdale Art Gallery, Lancashire, U.K.—The Bridgeman Art Library International **78** The Bloody Massacre by Paul Revere, 1770—The Gilder Lehrman Collection **79** Plate from W.D. Cooper. "Boston Tea Party.", The History of North America. London: E. Newberry, 1789—Art Resource, N.Y. **80** The Bostonians Paying the Excise-Man or Tarring & Feathering by Philip Dawe, London, 1774, Private Collection—Art Resource, N.Y. **81** (left) Granger Collection; Miriam and Ira D. Wallach Division of Art, Prints and Photographs. Astor, Lenox and Tilden Foundations—New York Public Library **82** Franklin Before The Lord's Council, Whitehall Chapel, London 1774, painted by C. Schuessele, engraved by Whitechurch—Library of Congress **84** (left) William Pitt the 'Elder', later 1st Earl of Chatham by William Hoare of Bath, Private Collection, Photo © Bonhams, London, U.K.—The Bridgeman Art Library International; Richard Howe, 1st Earl Howe, illustration from 'England's Battles by Sea and Land' by Lieut. Col. Williams (engraving) after Thomas Gainsborough, Private Collection, Ken Welsh—The Bridgeman Art Library International **85** Beinecke Rare Book and Manuscript Library, Yale University

CHAPTER 5

87 Granger Collection **88** Granger Collection **89** Granger Collection (2) **90** (left) Title page to 'Common Sense' by Thomas Paine, 1776, American Antiquarian Society, Worcester, Massachusetts, Bettmann Corbis **91** Granger Collection **92** Library of Congress **93** Congress Voting Independence by Robert Edge Pine and Edward Savage, c. 1795-1801, Atwater Kent Museum of Philadelphia, Historical Society of Pennsylvania Collection—The Bridgeman Art Library International **94** Passy et Chaillot, Vus

de Grenelle by Charles-Léopold Grevenbroeck, c.1740, Musée Carnavalet, Paris, Roger-Viollet—The Image Works **95** Map of Paris, 1736, Musee Conde, Chantilly, France, Lauros/Giraudon—The Bridgeman Art Library International **96** (top) Collection of the Grand Lodge of Free and Accepted Masons of Pennsylvania (Philadelphia, Pa.)—Photo by Peter Harholdt; Medallion from terra cotta casting by Jean Baptiste Nini, Photo by Arthur Feller, Benjamin Franklin Cabinet—Courtesy The Creativity Foundation **97** (clockwise from left) Count of Vergennes by Charles Gravier, 18th c., Chateau de Versailles, France, Lauros/Giraudon—The Bridgeman Art Library International; The British Museum; Granger Collection **98** Erich Lessing—Art Resource, N.Y. **99** Franklin's reception at the court of France, 1778, Lithograph, Library of Congress

CHAPTER 6

101 Portrait of Benjamin Franklin by Anne-Marie Bocquet Filleul, c. 1778-9, Philadelphia Museum of Art—Photo by Peter Harholdt **102** (left) John Adams by Mather Brown, 1788—Photo by Lee Bolton—Time Life Pictures; Library of Congress **103** Library of Congress **104** Library of Congress **105** Granger Collection **106** Library of Congress **107** Granger Collection (2) **108** (top to bottom) Granger Collection; The Potager of the Hôtel de Valentinois by Alexis Nicolas Pérignon the Elder, c. 1780, National Gallery of Art, Samuel H. Kress Collection, Stephen A. Schwarzman Building/Print Collection, Miriam and Ira D. Wallach Division of Art, Prints and Photographs—New York Public Library; American Philosophical Society **109** (clockwise from top left) Portrait of Voltaire by Catherine Lusurier, Chateau de Versailles, France—The Bridgeman Art Library International; Granger Collection; Louis XVI and members of the French royal family gathered around the dauphin born in 1781, Anonymous, c. 1782-1783. Chateaux de Versailles et de

Trianon, Versailles, Photo by Gérard Blot, Réunion des Musées Nationaux—Art Resource, N.Y. **110** American Philosophical Society—Photo by Peter Harholdt **111** (top) Publication of the Treaty of Versailles (Paris), signed between France and England before the Tuileries. November 25, 1783 by Anton Van Ysendyck, Photo by Gerard Blot, Réunion des Musées Nationaux—Art Resource, N.Y.; Osher Map Library and Smith Center for Cartographic Education at the University of Southern Maine **112** American Commissioners of the Preliminary Peace Negotiations with Great Britain, 1783-1785 by Benjamin West (attributed)—Winterthur Museum, Garden and Library **113** Granger Collection

CHAPTER 7

115 Second Street North from Market Street to Christ Church. Philadelphia, 1799, Drawn and engraved by W. Birch & Son—Art Resource, N.Y. **116** The Granger Collection **117** NOAA Photo Library **118** Drawing of Benjamin Franklin by Benjamin Franklin Bache (attributed)—American Philosophical Society **119** Edgar Fahs Smith Collection, Schoenberg Center for Electronic Text & Images, University of Pennsylvania Libraries **120** The Signing of the Constitution of the United States in 1787 by Howard Chandler Christy, 1940, Hall of Representatives, Washington, D.C.—The Bridgeman Art Library International **122** (top) Collection of the Grand Lodge of Free and Accepted Masons of Pennsylvania—Photo by Peter Harholdt (2); American Philosophical Society—Courtesy of The Benjamin Franklin Tercentenary **123** Medallion by William Hackwood, Josiah Wedgwood, c. 1787—American Philosophical Society **124** Joseph Sohn—Visions of America—Corbis **125** Beinecke Rare Book and Manuscript Library, Yale University **126** (left to right) Lester Lefkowitz—Getty Images; William Manning—Corbis; Lee Snider/Photo Images—Corbis; Stephen Finn—Alamy

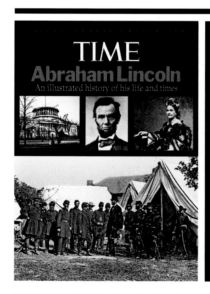